To Sizzle,
May the Lord bl
read this book

Find The TRUTH And Lock It In Your Heart

One Jew's Journey to the Messiah

REVD RALPH GOLDENBERG

'But when he, the ***Spirit of truth****, comes, he will guide you into all the truth. He will not speak on his own; he will speak only what he hears, and he will tell you what is yet to come. He will* ***glorify me*** *[Yeshua-Jesus] because it is from me that he will receive what he will make known to you.'*

(John 16:13-14)

Book production by www.creativebooksolutions.com
Printed in the United Kingdom

Contents

Introduction

'So Ralph, when are you going to write a book about your story?'

I have been asked that question many times, often by people who have heard me speak at a meeting or a conference. For some time now I have also felt a stirring in my spirit that God wants my story to be written.

Writing is certainly not one of my gifts. I can talk, no problem, but putting words onto paper is more of a challenge. So, when Jane Gibbs kindly offered to write my story in 2006, I agreed immediately. In fact, we spent a whole week's holiday with me talking and Jane writing. For many reasons that book was never published. However, it was a very helpful step towards writing this book. Thank you, Jane.

This year I suddenly felt that the time was right to focus on completing the book. When I finally finished writing everything down my wonderful, beautiful wife, Helen, agreed to read through and 'translate' my efforts into something more readable, filling in descriptive details I had omitted – a task made possible by our 50 years of married life. She has shared many of the experiences of my life and probably knows me better than anyone else. Thank you, my darling, for the many hours you spent.

My son, Olly, who has written a number of books himself (see www.childrencan.co.uk), also agreed to read and comment on the book. So this telling of my story is really a family affair.

As I wrote, I found myself reflecting on who the book is for and what is its main aim. I hope that telling the story of God working in my life to change me and guide me will bless and encourage others on their life's journey. Yeshua, Jesus, was and is a Jew who came first to the Jews. I am especially praying that this book will help other Jewish believers in their spiritual journey. *YHWH* is indeed alive and at work in our lives, through His Son Yeshua, by the power of *Ruach Hakodesh* – the Holy Spirit! I also pray that Gentile believers will be helped to have a better understanding of our Jewish roots, as seen through the eyes of a Jew.

Finally, I want to dedicate this book to my wife, Helen, who in many ways has co-authored this book, our three wonderful sons Mark, James and Olly, and our seven grandchildren. May you all be blessed as you discover more of our precious heritage.

Chapter 1
The Blessing of My Father

'Life is a journey with its ups and downs. There are times when we need to slow down because of traffic and other times to stop before proceeding. Those stop times can affect our whole life.'

Facing Jerusalem

Jewish people love a good argument. Opinions fly as thick and fast as there are people in the room. As we sat *shiva*[1] in Bournemouth after my father died, the debate was about which direction was East!

About fifteen family members and friends had squeezed into my father's room in the residential home where he and his wife, Irma (my stepmother), had been cared for over the past three months. The room was packed. The staff had done their best to make it suitable for the traditional Jewish mourning liturgy, moving furniture around and making space to accommodate the three low *shiva* chairs for Irma, my brother, Sol, and myself. By the time my wife, three sons, daughter-in-law, my sister's daughter, Rachel, and her husband had all come in, it was quite a squeeze.

The young, bearded, orthodox Rabbi, complete with black hat and ringlets, who was to conduct the funeral service swept into the room. He glanced around the room, silently counting heads to reassure himself that he had a *minyan* of ten men. Next he had to work around four different opinions as to where Jerusalem was. The argument grew more heated and he went out onto the landing to see where the sea was. Re-entering the room, he gestured eastward with his head. As he turned to face the prescribed direction, the men in their *kippas* and prayer shawls gathered standing behind him with their *sedur* prayer books open. At the far side of the room the women gathered around Irma.

The Rabbi started rattling his way through the beautiful Hebrew liturgy, including passages from Psalms and Deuteronomy. He began audibly, but was soon reciting almost silently. Only the rhythmical swaying of his body, the occasional 'Amen' or the turn of a page gave us any indication as to where he had reached. The liturgy became audible again as he reached the more familiar mourner's prayer, and as the Rabbi neared the end he started glancing over his shoulder to see if everyone else was keeping up. After a final 'Amen' the Rabbi turned towards Irma sitting on her low *shiva* chair. He bowed slightly and delivered the traditional greeting for such occasions: 'May you have good health and happiness and may we meet again in happier circumstances.' Then he was gone, leaving friends and family to comfort Irma.

Shiva

As he left, the traditional bagels and herring were produced for Irma, Sol and myself – designed to keep our strength up – and we started sharing our favourite memories of my father and grandfather to my children. The Jewish *shiva* allows seven days for friends and family to grieve and reminisce about the person they have lost.

A traditional Jewish story tells of two ships visible on the horizon, one setting off and one coming into harbour. Everyone cheers the outgoing ship, giving it a hearty send-off, while the other slips in almost unnoticed. So it is with birth and death: everyone celebrates a new birth, but dying is seen as a cause of sorrow.

'Rather ought the opposite to be the case. No one can tell what troubles await the child on its journey into manhood. But when a man has lived and dies in peace, all should rejoice, seeing that he has completed his journey and is departing this world with the imperishable crown of a good name.' (*A Book of Jewish Thoughts* – Dr J.H. Hertz, London 1917, p291)

The *shiva* is a healthy mechanism for the release of grieving, and I regret that there is no real counterpart in our Christian approach to mourning. Part of the ritual involved my brother, Sol, and myself having our shirts torn (yes, literally) by the rabbi to symbolise the cutting of death. This explains the derivation of Joel 2:13: '*Rend your hearts and not your garments, says the Lord.*' Various relatives suggested that I should wear a tatty old shirt, but I ignored them and bought a new one for the occasion. My Dad was worth it!

That same tearing of garments very often happens when someone in a Jewish family does what I did and becomes a Christian. It's symbolic of that person's death, effectively saying, 'The person alive now is not my son, but a stranger, for my son is dead.'

There are always poignant moments when someone close to us dies. But for me, sitting shiva for my father was full of extra significance. As I sat with Sol and Irma, as well as some of my father's friends from the local synagogue, the memories came thick and fast.

Rejected and Restored

I remembered clearly the day in the back room of my optical practice in January 1988 when I tried to explain to him that I felt the call into ministry in the Church of England. My becoming a Christian minister was even more difficult for him to accept than my acceptance of Jesus as Messiah. He was very upset; I had never seen him like that before.

'Never come to see me official'.

That was how he had put it in his broken English. In his mind's eye he saw me in the 'official' cassock worn by the Roman Catholic priests in the Sudan, the place of my childhood. There was no way he wanted ever to see me dressed up like that.

I remembered my own hurt over the next 7 years as Dad hardly spoke to me, despite the letters I'd written him telling him I still loved him. Telephone conversations were polite, but very brief. He never visited us in our home again. During my first curacy in Kinson, only a few miles from his home in Bournemouth, I hardly saw him.

By far my happiest memory during that *shiva* was the chain of events that started in 1995, when Paul Sands, the pastor of a neighbouring church, suggested we visit the Airport Church in Toronto. There had been a very special 'Father Heart move of God's Spirit' there and people were flocking to share in it from all over the world. We were on our way to a meeting. When we arrived, I called Helen from the office to suggest that we could join Paul on his trip to Toronto. In her quiet spiritual way she said, 'Of course, we should go.'

Before I knew it, Helen and I had joined Paul with our

churchwardens and their spouses from St Andrew's Church, Edgware, to fly to Toronto. Easter was approaching and it was a busy time to be leaving the church, but it felt like God was calling us to go. We travelled by Air India, the cheapest flight we could find.

'Why Toronto?' I asked the Lord during the flight over there. 'Why Bethlehem?' came the unmistakable answer! God is Sovereign.

At one of the worship evenings in the Toronto Airport Vineyard Church there was a specific invitation for Anglican pastors and their spouses to come forward to share testimony. 'That's for us!' said Helen. Helen told me afterwards that she was given a word by God that we would be sharing up front! After we shared our testimony we were prayed for.

As we were prayed for the Holy Spirit touched us both and we fell to the floor. If we didn't have a video of it, I would find it hard now to believe how we both fell in unison, holding hands together. Even our wardens and their spouses saw our synchronised fall to the floor as God flooded us with His Holy Spirit.

While I lay on the floor in the Lord's presence, I was given a picture of my father. He was on a bed, saying the *berakh* – the father's blessing – the most precious thing a father could give to his Jewish son. In reality, I was hardly even seeing my father, let alone receiving any form of blessing from him! I shared the vision with Helen and the rest of our group.

Arriving home, Barry Kissel invited me to speak at one of the monthly 'Catch the Fire' events at St Andrew's Church, Chorleywood. With holidays and other commitments it was six months before I was able to go.

I always say miracles are not simply an event, but an event

as a result of prayer or action in a specific *kairos* moment. Why did the sea divide at the moment when Moses lifted his hand, and not the day before or after? God's timing is always perfect. It was definitely God's timing that I was to speak at St Andrew's, Chorleywood on that Thursday in October.

I spoke about 'Joshua in the Torah' (Pentateuch) and specifically his vision of the Promised Land before he entered it. I shared what God had shown me in Toronto, stressing our need to faithfully claim God-given visions.

Three days later, on the Sunday, I had a distressing call from my stepmother Irma, to say that my father, aged 88, was seriously ill following a heart attack. I asked Irma if he would let me visit him and to my amazement she said, 'He wants to see you.' Helen and I hadn't moved so fast in a long time. We travelled from Edgware in London to Bournemouth in record time.

There were only two chairs next to Dad's bed (that seems to be the standard limit for chairs in UK hospitals). Irma and Helen sat in the chairs, leaving me to sit on the bed. Then Dad told us an incredible story.

On the previous Thursday night (the very night I'd spoken at Chorleywood) he'd had a dream. In it he saw vividly the time when he used to lay his hands on me and pray for me, and especially at my *Bar-Mitzvah*, when he laid his *tallet*[2] on my head and claimed me to be the 'son of the law' – *Bar Mitzvah.*

There was more. He believed that when he'd had his heart attack the previous day he had actually died. We were told by the nurses that his heart had indeed stopped for a time. During that time he had seen a bright light. He encountered some of his dead relatives and he heard a voice telling him to, 'Go back and fulfil the dream you had on Thursday.'

Now he wanted to give me his blessing. He laid his hands on my head and gave me his blessing, praying the Aaronic blessing in Hebrew:

Y'Berekha Adonai V Y'shmarecha (Numbers 6:24-26)...

'The Lord bless you and keep you; the Lord make his face shine on you and be gracious to you; the Lord turn his face toward you and give you peace.'

He continued, tearfully, and Helen remembers him whispering, 'I'm sorry.'

His words were unbelievable. It was a God-appointed moment that I will never forget. Seven years of pain and rejection melted away as we embraced each other. My prayers were answered: I had made peace with my father at last.

My dad made a good recovery and returned home. From that time we often used our day off to make the two-hour journey from London to Bournemouth to visit. When we later moved to Shrewsbury, it became a challenging four-hour drive each way. In the middle of busy ministry I would travel on my day off, often getting home around midnight and going straight into ministry commitments the following day.

Dad and Irma's favourite outing was a trip to Tesco in Bournemouth. Dad would ride in one of the supermarket's wheelchairs and sit beside me as we chatted over tea and scones or toasted teacakes in the cafeteria. I remember Dad once put his hand on my arm and said, 'It is good that we can talk together again.' As Dad became increasingly frail in his nineties, I would sit alone with him reminiscing, while Helen and Irma did the shopping. These were special times of healing.

Irma always had a definite plan for her shopping. She would buy things in the order they were written on the list. This meant Helen and Irma would rush from one end of the shop to the other and back again several times on each trip. Helen soon got to know what was needed and where to find it. She mastered finding the Kosher section, too, when Jewish festivals were approaching. Having safely negotiated the checkout, Helen and Irma would then retreat to the cafeteria to join us for tea and scones and to rest their feet.

The End of an Era

It was 5 years later, in October 2000, that we nearly lost him again. But he rallied and on the 5th of October 2002 we had a joint family celebration for his 95th birthday, Irma's 85th birthday and their 30th anniversary which was coming up at the end of that month. We organised lunch in a local restaurant and all our sons took time off to be there. Mark came from Yorkshire, James from Bournemouth, and Olly and his wife, Helen, came down from London. It was so good to all be together. Dad and Irma thoroughly enjoyed themselves and ate more than we had seen them manage for a long time. The photos we have are a happy reminder of a family re-united.

Little did we know that the next time we would all be together would be in just two months' time for Dad's funeral.

Just before he died, Dad made a specific and very meaningful request: would I sit *shiva* and say the *kaddish* for him (the Jewish mourners' prayer said by the relative of a deceased person, especially the son)? I was thrilled. It felt like a final affirmation of his acceptance of me. 'Of course I would, Dad,' I replied.

A couple of weeks after this, not long before Christmas, a telephone call came from the residential home. Dad had been admitted to hospital with another heart attack. Helen and I packed an overnight bag and jumped in the car straight away.

When we arrived at the hospital, Dad was resting comfortably, but the next day, when we saw him for the last time, he was rather agitated and tearful. I sat with him, reassuring him that I loved him. I held his hand and Helen stroked his hair. We both prayed silently for him until he became peaceful and drifted off to sleep. It was three days after Christmas when he died.

Some time later a Christian friend believed he heard a word from the Lord for me about 7 years of famine and 7 years of plenty – like the dream Joseph had in Egypt. I found myself wondering whether that might have been why Dad didn't die in 2000, at the first false alarm. Either way, I am just delighted that the Lord was gracious enough to give us those 7 years of plenty before the end.

Endnotes

1. *Shiva* is the structured mourning that Jews go through following the death of a close relative.
2. A *Tallet* is the name given to the prayer shawls that the Jews use while praying. It can be placed over other people as you pray blessings on them.

Chapter 2
My Jewish Roots

My Maternal Grandparents

Once, when we were leaving Israel I was stopped at security. The security person asked, 'Why were you born in the Sudan?' After a short pause, I could think of no better answer than, 'Because my mother was there!' If she had gone on to ask why my mother was there I would have had no choice but to say, 'Because my grandparents were there when she was born!'

The story of why my grandfather went to the Sudan is interesting. Professor Warburg in his article[1] describes how my grandfather ended up there. He included pictures of both my grandparents: Chief Rabbi Solomon Malka, 1906-1949, and his wife, Rubisa Hanna. He also included pictures of the synagogue in the Sudan where I worshipped.

The Mahdi was ruler and spiritual leader of the Sudanese from the mid 19th Century. Towards the end of the century he went to his friend, General Gordon, and stated that according to his Islamic faith Gordon was an infidel, and so killed him. In response, Queen Victoria and the British Government sent a large Anglo-Egyptian army under the command of General Kitchener, who in the great battle of Khartoum, managed to defeat the Mahdi and bring peace to Sudan.

During the Mahdi's rule, the Jews were forced to convert

to Islam and marry Moslem women. When the Mahdi was removed they reverted to their Jewish roots. They wrote to the Jewish Seminary in Safed near Tiberias and asked for a Rabbi to be sent to them to teach and revitalise their faith. My grandfather, Solomon Malka, and his young wife, Hanna, came to lead that Jewish community. In time he became Chief Rabbi of the whole area. They were Sephardic in origin and spoke Ladino (Hebrew Spanish). The synagogue followed the Sephardic tradition.

In his book, *A Legacy of Faith and Tolerance*, my uncle, David Malka, summarises some of my grandfather's teaching and has many stories of our family. He even names all the Malka children, including my mother, Rachel.

One of the many interesting stories he wrote included one about his mother (my grandmother) which describes something of the Jewish life in Sudan:

'The Rubisa was also the centre of Jewish family life. She was consulted regularly on rituals by her women friends. Our house had the only 'Mikvah' (baptistery) and every bride-to-be was brought to the Rubisa for the ritual cleansing, followed by a great party and much rejoicing. As a little boy I remember being chased out on those occasions.'

My grandparents had around 40 grandchildren, yet somehow seemed to know them all. Or at least, whenever I sat on my grandfather's lap he seemed to know me even though his sight was going. I have memories of sitting on his lap and touching his long white beard. I loved it when he laid hands on my head and prayed over me.

One time he prayed over me in Arabic:

'Seek the truth and lock it in your heart.'

Looking back, I can say I certainly did find the truth: *Yeshua*

Amashia. Jesus, my Messiah.

Chief Rabbi Solomon Malka was highly respected by all in the community and all who knew him. I am told that his funeral was attended by bishops and other dignitaries. At the age of four I was too young then to be aware of such niceties. My memories of him were that of a gentle, holy, role model. He was a wonderful storyteller and I used to be mesmerised by him.

My grandfather also invested in young Rabbis known as Talmidim. In David H. Stern's Jewish New Testament, a Talmid or disciple is defined as follows:

'The relationship between a Talmid and his Rabbi was very close; not only did the Talmid learn facts, reasoning processes and how to perform religious practices, but he regarded him as an example to be imitated in conduct and character. The Rabbi in turn was considered responsible for his Talmidim.'

This definition of Talmid explains the intimate relationship between Jesus and His disciples. My grandfather was not only keen to equip the next generation of Rabbis, but also was very open to discussing faith. He met regularly with other faith leaders including the Catholic priest.

I am often asked, 'As a Jew, what did you think of the Holy Spirit?' (*Rouach Hakodesh*). In another book about my grandfather, *Frontiers of the Jewish Faith*, another uncle, Edmond Malka, wrote about my grandfather's teaching on Genesis 1 and 2.

'Chief Rabbi Malka raises the question regarding whether the Lord finished creating the world in 6 days (Gen.1) or 7 days (Gen.2:1-3) and answers it as follows:

"The first question is answered by the fact that a body, devoid of soul, is liable to decomposition. It's only the existence of a soul that prevents disintegration. What actually happened is that creation was, in fact, completed at the end of the sixth day. But it was only when the Sabbath arrived, that (*Rouach Hakodesh*) the Holy Spirit was instilled to sanctify the objects created.'"

I fully agree that without the Holy Spirit a person or a church is not spiritually alive 'and is liable to decomposition and disintegration'. We need God the Holy Spirit in us and in our churches to grow.

I spoke to my mother mainly in Arabic and when she left Sudan in 1958 we continued to correspond in Arabic. One of the most precious books I inherited was my grandfather's *Tenach* (Old Testament) in Arabic.

My Paternal Family

Growing up I heard very little about my Dad's parents. Years later, as I sat in Tesco with him, while my wife Helen ran around the shop with my stepmother, Irma, he shared some of his childhood and I began to understand him better. My paternal grandfather was apparently born in Romania to a rabbinic family. He later moved to Cairo to start an optical practice which he passed on to his eldest son. Sadly, following my father's birth, my paternal grandmother was sectioned and taken into a psychiatric ward, possibly because of post-natal depression. Poor Dad had to be fostered from the age of two. I grew up thinking I had an Italian grandmother (yet another language to add to my repertoire), when in reality she was my Dad's *foster* mother.

My father (1907-2002) was the youngest of 7 children and grew up in Cairo. His parents were Ashkenazi Jews who spoke Yiddish (Hebrew German). Although he was only 5' 2", Dad was grossly overweight most of his life, and when he retired to Bournemouth in 1970 he weighed around 22 Stone. He surprised us all by managing to slim down to 12 Stone. Then he surprised us again by marrying Irma, his second wife, in 1972 when he was 65.

My father was trained as an optician in Cairo by his oldest brother and obtained a diploma from Switzerland by correspondence. His brother encouraged him to relocate to Khartoum to set up his own practice. Naturally, he joined the Jewish community in my grandfather's synagogue, and it was there that he set eyes on the rabbi's beautiful daughter, Rachel. They married in 1932 and their first child, Adolph, was born the following year. As I mentioned, two of Dad's sisters married two of my mother's brothers, so these three families were related through both parents.

Over the years, the Jewish community grew in numbers under my grandfather's ministry. Sadly, there are now no Jews left in the Sudan. On the Internet the following is written:

The fading frontage of Maurice Goldenberg's shop in Khartoum is the only proof that Jews once lived and thrived in Sudan under British colonial rule. There were almost 1,000 Jews, Sephardi as well as Ashkenazi. Today there are none. They and their descendants are scattered between the US, Israel, Switzerland and the UK.[2]

There is even a picture of my father's shop on this web page.

I spoke to my father both in Arabic and French, as he went to the French School in Cairo. At the age of 13, as a boarder in school, I started to study Italian with the Catholic priests. Italian was also one of my father's languages that somehow got thrown in the mix of languages whenever we spoke. My father also spoke *Yiddish* (German Hebrew) and often threw *Yiddish* phrases into our conversations as well.

Memories of Growing up With a Large Jewish Family

I have so many wonderful memories from my childhood. One of the special memories is of visiting my grandmother, Rubisa Hanna, who towards the end of her life, lived with her youngest daughter, my favourite Aunt, Vicky. As she lay on her bed and we chatted she reminded me that my name, Raphael ben Moshe, means 'God's healing man'. *Rophe* is Hebrew for 'healing' and El Hebrew for 'God'. Moshe (Moses) is, of course, 'waters', representing the Holy Spirit. She also told me, 'Make sure you fulfil all God has called you to be.'

Another time my grandmother said similar words to those my grandfather prayed over me. *'Shoof al hagiga wa agfila fi galbak'* – 'Look for the truth and when you find it, lock it in your heart.' Years later, when I came to know Jesus as my Messiah, those words became reality for me. As Jesus said in John 14:6, 'I am the way and the truth and the life. No one comes to the Father except through me.'

That search would not begin in earnest for a while. In the meantime, I loved being part of a large family. When I was young, I played with my many cousins, especially Monie and David. We were all similar ages and enjoyed being together. When they moved away to the USA and Israel, they left a gap in my life. For a season, my favourite Aunty Vicky and her two children came and lived with us. Her daughter, Valery, was a similar age to me, so we played many games together. They also moved away to live in Spain for a time, then moved on to America.

My Brothers and Sister

Adolph: My eldest brother, Adolph, was 12 years older than me. While I was still a young boy he went to the UK for further studies and when he came back, he only remained for a short while before emigrating to the USA, where he taught in high school. He married Mary and they settled in Atlanta where they raised their family, Joseph, Jo-Ann and little Adolph (Dolph). We heard at one point that he had become a Christian Scientist and changed his surname to Goldenburg. I remember thinking, 'How could he? After all, we are Jews!' God must have smiled at that thought!

As a family, we visited Atlanta and stayed with Adolph and his family. We had a great time with them. The children enjoyed playing together with their transatlantic cousins. Sadly he passed away 15 years ago.

Claudette: My sister is 9 years older than me. I shared a bedroom with her – until she got married – and my brother, Solomon, who was 5 years older than me. I always looked up to Solomon, even though he used to tease me a lot. One day my sister arrived home. Sol said, 'Come and look through the window, someone's hair is on fire!' When I looked I saw a red haired man, Yacov, with my sister (they subsequently married).

Claudette and Yacov had a daughter, Rachel. I got to hold her in my arms when she was a tiny baby. In her early thirties Rachel had a strong faith in Yeshua. Sadly, she recently passed away at the age of 60. She had been ill for several years.

I presided at her funeral service in Basildon some months ago. She was ill, but she knew the Lord and He was her strength. With her second husband Claudette had two further children, David and Esther.

Solomon: Sol is 5 years older than me. He was very bright and at the young age of 15 achieved 12 O-Levels. He went on to study medicine in Khartoum. In the mid-1960s he came to the UK and passed the MBBS when he was only 22. He practiced medicine until he retired. He married Annette and they had one daughter, Lisa, and also have a granddaughter, Natalie. Sol and all his family now live in Florida.

My dad often tried to compare our academic achievements and I remember when I was doing my A-Levels in Brighton he said, 'Look at your brother. At your age he already won a Prize at the medical school.' I pointed out in reply that I was normal doing four A-Levels at the age of 18!

Growing up in Khartoum, Sudan

Growing up in Khartoum was very different from my life now in England. The culture was different in so many ways. The weather in Sudan is very hot, and can reach up to 40 degrees Centigrade. The menfolk all lived in shorts and short-sleeved tops and the women wore colourful cotton dresses. The local Arab men wore their cool *Jellabiya* and the Arab women wore *Hijab*, fully covered except for their eyes. Walking in the streets was dusty and rough, especially shopping in the *souk*. When I first came to England I noticed that the men didn't hold hands, but the women did – exactly the opposite of what I'd been used to in the Sudan. Not only that, but the women also wore miniskirts!

My parents owned three neighbouring houses and we lived in the biggest one. The large front veranda led to three rooms: a large lounge/dining room, mum and dad's bedroom and our bedroom. At the back was another veranda – a covered one where we had our meals. This led to the bathroom, kitchen and servant-bedroom. We had proper plumbing in the house by the time I was born, but previously the toilet had been outside and this one was still in use. It operated on a bucket system below a hole in the ground, collected nightly by an open lorry.

The lorry rang a bell to announce its arrival. I could never work out why they bothered, you could tell it was coming just by the smell. Looking back, it was obviously a warning to anyone who was using the toilet that their personal space was about to be invaded!

We had a courtyard at the back of the house where I often played, with a tree that I loved climbing. We even had a garage for our posh Vanguard car. We slept upstairs on the open veranda, which was partly covered for us, to shelter under when it rained. Some nights the rain seemed to come so suddenly. It was funny whenever we had to get up in the middle of the night to move our beds under the covered veranda because of the rain.

As a Jew in an Arab country, I found my company mainly within our family, though that was large enough to give plenty of scope. I did have some wonderful Arab Moslem friends and Christian friends who came from South Sudan. The Jewish Recreation Club in Khartoum was the centre of meeting for all of us youngsters. All celebrations and parties, such as wedding receptions and Bar Mitzvah, took place in that club. We had children's parties and so much fun. In time, there were fewer parties and celebrations as more and more Jews left the country.

The parties were truly joyful events with dancing, singing, eating and drinking. Dancing with my well-endowed aunts as I grew up was a challenge. I was never sure where to put my face as they pulled me close to them!

Sudan was given Independence on 1st January, 1956, and became the 'Republic of Sudan'. It was governed by a Moslem Parliament. Following the Arab-Israeli war of October/November 1956, it became more difficult for the Jewish community to remain in the Sudan. Therefore, sadly, over time more and more of my family and friends left the Sudan and the recreation club was sold.

Nowadays the word 'Sudan' summons up a picture of desperate famine and war-stricken hopelessness. Nothing could have been further from what I remember of my time growing up there during the 1950s and 60s. We were comfortably off, with servants to cook meals and clean the house. If anything, I was over fed and had the feeling that mum showed her love for me by feeding me to excess. As a child I got so fat that people used to call me '*Baffo al Samien*' – 'Ralph the fatty'.

One day, one of my aunts who had a son that looked a bit like me, smacked me on the head. She then realised I was not her son and said '*O Baffo al Samien*, I thought you were my son!' I wondered why her son was never called fat like me?

I was also bullied quite a lot at school, especially when I became a boarder in 1958. '*Shouf al Yahudi al Samien*' – 'Look at the fat Jew.' One day, I was playing basketball when someone pushed me over and laughed, saying, '*Yehudi al Samien.*' Fat Jew! It was hurtful at the time. Even now, when I remember those times, I ask Jesus to heal me of the pain.

I had a Moslem live-in nanny by the name of Salamtu, who was an important figure in my young life. She told me stories of al-Mahdi and about the Islamic Sharia laws, some of which I found difficult to grasp. As a child, I could not understand why you would want to cut the hand off a thief or whip someone. However, whenever I was lonely or sad I would go to the servant's room where she slept and found much comfort in talking to her. Often, as I sat there, she would tell me some wonderful children's stories. When I went to boarding school I missed her so much. By the time I came home again I lived in another house, without Salamtu.

My childhood was one of great joy with my family, but also one where I gathered many hurts and suffered many losses. My greatest pain did not come from the other children teasing me at school, however, it came from within my family.

Endnotes

1. His article can be seen here: www.academy.ac.il/SystemFiles/21077.pdf, accessed 7th March 2017.

2.http://jewishrefugees.blogspot.co.uk/2012/11/the-jews-took-their-dead-with-them-out.html

Chapter 3
Growing Up With Pain

Mum's Accident

Not all my childhood memories are happy ones. In 1949, after her father's death, Mum was involved in a major car accident. Doctors told my dad that they did not expect her to survive. If she did somehow pull through, they said her back had been broken and she would be unable to walk. My father paid for her to be treated in the UK. She had long-term treatment in a plaster bed in Middlesex Hospital. I travelled to the UK to visit her. As I saw her lying on the plaster bed, I wondered if my mum would ever be back to normal. That night I curled up in my bed and cried. I was only five years old and I could not really understand what was happening. All I knew was that my mum was no longer the same as she had been.

In 1950 we came back to the Sudan without her. It seemed a long time before she came home again. As a five year old I often went to Salamtu asking, 'When is Mum coming back? Will she be OK?' Finally, she came home and, miraculously, she was able to walk, cook and organise the household once again.

Mum told me that one night while she was asleep in her hospital bed, she had a dream that my grandfather came to her and anointed her with oil for healing. When she awoke the next morning, her nightdress was covered with oil.

Locked Up

From when I was twelve years old, my parents frequently quarrelled. One time my mother got so angry that she picked up oranges and threw them at my dad. The arguing went from bad to worse and so I was sent to be a boarder at Comboni College.

Comboni College was founded and run by the Roman Catholic Italian Verona Fathers. I had attended as a day boy since the age of five. All my brothers and male cousins went through this school and the girls went to a separate school run by nuns. As Jews, we were exempt from all Catholic Christian acts of worship. Everyone knew we were Jewish.

I was a boarder for 2 terms in 1958. Most daytimes there were okay, as I was busy studying and playing basketball, but the rest of the time it was not so pleasant. My private space was my bed and a small cupboard. The room was shared with eleven other children. Some were Christians, mainly from South Sudan. They were always polite and helpful. Others were not so kind, as I mentioned before. By this time, many of my close cousins had left Sudan. It was not a pleasant experience and often I went to sleep feeling lonely and unhappy.

Every Saturday I was allowed to go to the synagogue where I would receive special teaching from the Rabbi in preparation for my Bar Mitzvah. This key event was my transition into adulthood. For the Jews, it is as big a celebration as a wedding day.

During that time my dad would visit me almost every lunchtime with tears in his eyes. He no longer bubbled with joy. Now that I understand his story better, I can see why he radiated sadness. During this time I hardly saw my mum. Although my brother, Sol, came to visit, his visits were only occasional and too brief for my liking. All in all, it was a lonely time for me. The worst day was when Sol came to tell me that Mum had been arrested and taken to prison. I never knew all the details, but I understood that it had to do with the three neighbouring properties we owned. These were part of Mum's dowry, given when my parents got married. By now my parents were in the middle of a messy divorce. Because of the divorce proceedings, it was ordered the properties were not to be sold until a financial agreement had been reached, which was ignored. My dad officially released the properties to her and she was let out the next day.

Imagine my confusion as a 13-year-old, with all this happening while I was away at boarding school, with no close friends for support. My family, that had been at the centre of my early childhood, was now being torn to pieces.

I often burst into tears when I went to see the Rabbi. He was my one source of strength at this time. On one occasion, as I spent time with the Rabbi, we were looking at the wonderful prayer said between *Rosh Hashanah* (New Year) and *Sukkot* (Tabernacles) – a prayer of forgiveness which contains the words, '*Avinu malkeinu sh'ma kolenu.*' – Our Father our King, hear our voice.' This triggered strong emotions in me. 'Heavenly Daddy, where are you? Why are you not hearing my voice and my pain?' I cried out. This led to another round of tears. The poor Rabbi had to sit through all this. To this day, tears well up in my eyes whenever I hear that song.

My time as a boarder came to an end at the start of the summer holiday in 1958 and in the autumn term I returned to school as a day boy. For the next four years my dad and I lived in a small, two-bedroom house with a veranda in Khartoum, on the outskirts of the capital. We had a live-in servant girl who cooked our meals and kept the house clean. But Salamtu, my second mother, was gone! Often I came home to an empty house as dad worked long hours.

Bar Mitzvah

As I approached the age of thirteen, I looked forward to my *Bar Mitzvah* (which mean, 'son of the law'), when I officially became a man according to Jewish understanding. I was now able to sit with the men in the synagogue. In fact, I can still visualise my place in the synagogue, next to dad. As a man, I could put on my *Tallit* (prayer shawl) and *Tephilin* (prayer boxes worn on the forehead and the arms as prescribed in Deuteronomy 6:4-9). These verses are known as the *Shema*: 'Hear O Israel' – a statement central to Jewish belief and practice. From that day, I was able to be counted as one of the *minyan* – the ten men required to form a synagogue for prayer.

The prayers recited when putting on both the *Tallit* and *Tephilin* are very powerful.

In putting on the *Tallit*, you say, 'You commanded us to enwrap ourselves in fringed garments and find refuge in the shadow of Your wings.' Those words meant a lot to me. As I wrapped myself in my prayer shawl I found refuge in God.

The prayers when putting on the *Tephilin*, 'Blessed are you, Lord God, who commanded us concerning the precept of the Tephilin' brought the meaning of a Creator God alive. The box covering my head (*rosh*) signified filling my mind with God. Then the box on my left arm, next to my heart, was where I wanted God to be in my heart.

As Deuteronomy 30:6 says, *'The* LORD *your God will circumcise your hearts and the hearts of your descendants, so that you may love him with all your heart and with all your soul, and live.'*

I was confused by the prayer said when winding the *Tephilin* three times round my middle finger: *'God says, "I will betroth you to Me forever in righteousness and justice with love and mercy with faithfulness and you shall know the Lord."'* Wow! God marrying me in love and mercy while winding the *Tephilin* three times. Why three? Today I think of my betrothal to the Triune God, Father, Son and Holy Spirit.

The young adult's *Bar Mitzvah* is meant to be one of the most joyful times of celebration, but the run up to mine was full of arguments between my parents. They even fought over who should buy my suit! However, on the day of the Bar Mitzvah there was a sense of peace as I got up to read from the Torah holding the *Yad* (a metal hand) with which I pointed to every word as I read it from the Sepher containing the sacred texts. The party that followed lacked many of our extended family, including my favourite cousins, Monie and David, who had already left Sudan. I felt lonely. How can one feel alone with people around them? It is easy when there is no one close to share with in a real way.

Some of my friends thought I had become very religious, saying my daily prayers, going to the synagogue regularly and doing everything I could to follow the Jewish faith. One of my friends even asked if I was going to become a Rabbi. Little did they know what God had in store for me as in due course I would become a teacher (rabbi), teaching God's Word to His people.

Freedom

When my parents finally divorced, I was shocked. In spite of all the arguments, divorce was something that Jewish parents simply did not do in those days. Like many children caught up in divorce, I prayed fervently that God would bring them back together. It didn't happen. When my mum left, I do not even remember her saying goodbye to me. She didn't just leave our home, she emigrated to America to live with my eldest brother, Adolph. Life went on without Mum.

In 1959, a new Jewish boy, Isaac Shalom, joined the school. His father had moved to Sudan to be the CEO of a large company. Isaac was in the same year, in the same top class as me. This boy became what I needed at that time, a best friend. God sent him to me. Kino, as I came to know him, had a laid back, peaceful character – truly the Shalom friend I needed.

Kino's mother was a beautiful petite French woman. She was very warm and welcoming and often invited me to eat with their family. I looked to her for the motherly care that was now missing from my life. The hardest part of my childhood was now past and I was discovering a 'new normal' in life. Although I was often sad in those days from all that I had been through, it was not all tinged with sadness.

At the age of sixteen I passed my driving test and moved into a new era of independence. I drove my father's big Vanguard car around town. Then one day my father bought me a little green car of my own, a Standard 10. It was the love of my life. With it I could get to school much more easily. I also had so much fun travelling around with my friends in that little car.

We used to sing and laugh as I drove the car, with as many friends as I could pack into it. One day I was stopped by a policeman.

'How many friends have you got in that car?' he asked.

'Six,' I replied.

He frowned at me and suggested that in future I should keep it to 4!

I had a new-found freedom to enjoy life. Soon it would be my time to travel even further as I followed the example of many others in my family and left Sudan for good.

Chapter 4
Coming to the UK

Shifting Gears

'What profession do you want to have? What do you want to study for?' my dad asked.

'I'll think about it,' I said.

Many thoughts crossed my mind, from becoming an engineer to a marine biologist, but I couldn't shake the thought that I was to, 'follow the family line.' The question was, which line? Should I be a Rabbi or an Optician? I opted for the latter. I was already helping in my father's shop by cutting and fitting lenses to frames, especially for the 'rimless' ones that were popular at the time and needed holes drilled on the edges.

I really enjoyed watching my dad examining people's eyes with familiar questions like, 'Which is better, one or two?' Without too much more thought I told Dad I wanted to follow in his footsteps and become an optician. I could feel his joy as he offered me a choice of where to study.

According to Dad, the best courses were available in Germany, the USA or the UK. Kino had also been considering his future and had decided to study for his A-Levels in Whittingham College, a Jewish school in Brighton, before attending a UK university. So my decision was made to go to the UK: first, Whittingham College with Kino to do my A-Levels, and then on to study to be an optician. So it was that in 1962, aged 17, Kino and I arrived together at Whittingham College.

The boarding accommodation was full and as sixth-formers we were considered to be responsible, so we were put in a local vicar's house with a number of rules that we were supposed to keep. We were not allowed to cook in the vicarage, but one day Kino decided to cook spaghetti Bolognese. That probably would have been alright if the sauce had not splattered over the whole kitchen. The vicar came in as we were still clearing up the after effects of our culinary attempts.

We were also supposed to be home at a set time. For both Kino and me, the night life was too exciting to drag ourselves away and we were frequently late home. Life was so different from Sudan. The mini-skirt had just come in and the pretty girls who wore them were a real distraction from our studies and responsibilities.

I arrived in the UK weighing over 17.5 Stone (*Baffo al Samin*, Fat Ralph). I decided I needed to lose weight. I began to eat just one meal at lunchtime, every other day, jog, and play tennis in Surrenden Park. Very quickly, within a few months, I came down to 12 Stone. Weight has always been and continues to be a problem for me. I like to claim it is genetic, as both my parents were overweight, but it may also have something to do with the fact that I overeat and don't exercise enough.

Whittingham College was multinational, with Jewish boys from all around the world and acted in part to prepare non-English students for university entrance in the UK. My first challenge was to learn enough English to pass the English O-Level which was an entry requirement of every university in the UK. It took a few attempts and some memorising of essays, but I passed English Language and my combined

Maths A-Level in January 1964. Then, in July 1964, I passed separate Maths and Physics A-Levels with the required grades to enter the City University in London to study Ophthalmic Optics, as it was known at the time. Now the profession is called Optometry.

Looking back, I can see God's hand on me during my time at Whittingham College. Our headmaster was Mr Levy, a Jew, but the deputy head was Mr Smith, known by all his students as *Shmats*. He was loved by all and there was something special about him. In fact, when he died some years ago, many of his past students with whom he kept in touch wanted to celebrate and give thanks for his life, and his input into all our lives. I discovered some years ago, when we were having a telephone conversation, that he was a strong Christian and that his daughter had become a Methodist minister. I find it interesting that once more I was living in a Christian place (in the vicarage) and had a Christian deputy head who undoubtedly prayed for me.

These were carefree days, but the parting of the ways for my friend and I came all too soon. In 1964 Kino went to Bangor University to study electronics and I went to the City University in London. We lost touch. It would not be until 2003, through *Shmats*, that I would catch up with Kino again. By then he was living in Nice, France, and as I was often visiting that area we were able to meet up. Forty years just evaporated and we were like young teenagers all over again, enjoying the chance to reminisce over our shared past.

Meeting and Marrying my Wonderful Wife

During my second term, while I was still 19, Helen caught my eye from across a dance floor at the City University. She was a fellow optometry student, but a year older than me and in her final year. She was a blue-eyed, blonde, Anglo-Saxon beauty (and more than 50 years on she still is). One look at her retina and I was captivated! Before long we were together.

As time went by I discovered that there was much more to Helen than blue eyes and blonde hair. I realised that she was very bright too. She brought with her a peace and healing to my insecurities and wounds. Her upbringing was very different from mine. She grew up in a stable family in the UK. All who meet her say that she blesses them. I thank God for bringing us together.

Shortly after my 20th birthday we were engaged. We were very aware of our different religious and cultural roots and family backgrounds, so the question of where to get married was a real dilemma. Helen had just graduated, but I still had two more years to go, so we decided to wait until I also graduated. This gave us plenty of time to talk things through and explore our options. Neither of us favoured the registry office, because we both instinctively wanted God's blessing on our marriage.

I had never doubted the existence of God, but most of my Jewish tradition had been left behind in Sudan. I did not even go to the synagogue any more. Helen was what I now laughingly call, 'C and E' (rarely darkening the door of any church apart from Christmas and Easter). She had a basic belief in who Jesus was, so it was out of the question for her to convert to Judaism.

Helen's mother had sadly been widowed 6 months earlier. She worshipped in her local Anglican Church, St Anne's Bagshot. We decided to explore the possibility of getting married there, so we made an appointment with the vicar. Looking back, we can see God's hand was upon us all those years ago. The vicar was very welcoming and gracious and his counsel kept many doors open for us. He was happy to marry us, he said, on the grounds of Helen's nominal belief as a confirmed member of the Anglican faith and her residence in the parish.

He went through the liturgy of the marriage service with us, saying he was happy for me to omit any words that would compromise my Jewish beliefs. What this boiled down to was the words 'Jesus' or 'The Son'. I don't think anyone noticed my not saying those words.

He also said that he would rather our children were brought up in the Jewish faith than not to know God at all. His graciousness towards us was a great encouragement at this stage of our relationship. Then he spoke some words that struck to the very heart of my spiritual journey: 'Search for the truth and follow wherever it leads you.' He did not know it, but these words reminded me of the very words both my grandfather and grandmother had spoken over me: 'Search for the truth and lock it in your heart.'

This was not a search that I was ready to pursue yet. With wedding plans fully underway and our whole lives together ahead of us, our focus was on other things. So it was that on July 29th, 1967, we were married in the church and started our new life together. We both secured jobs in Bournemouth, in the same family-run optical practices, and we purchased our first home in Highcliffe, a brand new mid-terrace, two-up two-down.

My Time at the City University

I struggled with my English at university and as a result failed some exams in my first year. As I discussed my exam papers with Helen, I realised how my lack of understanding of English was a barrier to my passing the exams. For example, one question said to draw Schlemm's Canal (a circular vessel in the eye). Helen asked how many of the layers I had managed to label.

'Label? There was no mention of that in the question,' I told her. I had simply drawn it as the question had asked. I had to learn that if I was asked to draw something, it meant that I needed to label it as well. If only I had understood that before; I could easily have labelled every layer we were taught.

The Principal at the time was Professor Fletcher, another wonderful Christian who I am sure was also praying for me. At the end of the summer he invited me to take some re-sits, which I passed and so I continued with the course. For my final exams – of which there were many, written, practical and *viva voce* (oral) – again I had to do a retake of one viva. With this final hurdle passed, I achieved my FBOA – Fellow of the British Optical Association – in December 1967.

Two Ophthalmic Practices

I started my pre-registration year in September 1967 with a small company called Springate Ltd., in Boscombe, Bournemouth. Mr Springate was my supervisor. After achieving my FBOA and completing my pre-registration year, I was registered in 1968 with the GOC (General Optical Council). Once registered, I was keen to either be in a partnership or have my own business, rather than work for a company, so when I saw an advert to work for Bert Hatfield in his practice in Parkstone, with the possibility of a partnership, I applied immediately.

Bert had established and run his practice in a house opposite shops, on part of the high street. There was more demand for his services than he could manage on his own, and there was much scope for expansion.

Bert and Marie Hatfield were wonderful Christians and active members of the local Methodist church. They were lovely people and treated Helen and me as part of their family. Once again, another wonderful Christian person entered my life and modelled something good of the Christian faith.

Bert and I got on really well together and after a short trial period we became partners. I remember when we were discussing our partnership, how we tried to see each other's point of view. Bert was nearing retirement age and a few years later when he retired I became sole proprietor. Coincidentally, a retail premises came up for sale just across the road and we moved the optical practice into it.

By then Helen and I had moved to Ferndown to be closer to work, and had started a small, very part-time practice in our home. The local health authority were about to build a new health centre in the middle of Ferndown, and approached us to offer us a suite of rooms there. We jumped at the opportunity and a couple of years later moved our second practice there.

By the age of 35 I was success story in the eyes of the world. I owned two thriving optical practices and had eight staff. I was Chairman of the National OBVA (Orthoptic and Binocular Vision Association), was elected on the FPC Ophthalmic Committee, and was secretary and chairman of the local AOP (Association of Optical Practitioners).

We then moved again, staying in Ferndown, to our 'forever' family home – a lovely 1930s neo-Georgian style house set in half an acre. Over the years, we made improvements and additions, including a swimming pool and tennis court. We had everything anyone could want materially.

Three Boys to Love

Things were good on the family front too. Problems with conceiving a baby early on in our marriage had led to our adopting Mark at 7 months old. Whenever I preach on us being adopted children of God, I am reminded of holding Mark in my arms as a baby and the love that I had for him. Mark has always been as much our son as our two 'home grown' sons. When God adopts us as His children, we are not second rate children. We are held in God's arms and receive His love.

We loved parenthood, so you can imagine our delight when Helen eventually became pregnant, three years after adopting Mark. We had a few anxious days when her blood pressure went out of control, and labour had to be induced five weeks early, two days before Christmas. Mark, the turkey, and all the presents, went over to Helen's mother, who was now living just a mile away. I stayed with Helen for the thirty-three hours of labour, pacing the corridor when she disappeared into theatre for a Caesarean section.

Ten minutes before Christmas day, on Christmas Eve 1973, James arrived. He was healthy, but tiny, weighing a mere 3lbs 6ozs (1.53 kg). When we brought him home, after five weeks in special care, the first thing Mark, now aged four, said was, 'He is not a bit like a rabbit!' We were puzzled for a moment. We were sure he knew he was getting a baby brother, not a pet rabbit. Eventually we remembered that my mother-in-law had popped into special care to see James on Christmas day. She had returned to Mark and announced that James was tiny, just like a little skinned rabbit. It seems Mark was convinced from that moment that his new brother was a rabbit!

Two years later Oliver (or Olly, as he likes to be known), was born. Our family was complete. Olly has his own wonderful story of his journey with God, as he now leads an international ministry. To find out how God is using him, visit his website: www.childrencan.co.uk.

I had everything I could have ever wanted – except that there was a spiritual emptiness in my heart. I was now ready to seek the truth.

Chapter 5
Making the Connection

Starting the Journey of Finding the Truth

After ten years of marriage we had everything we had ever hoped and dreamed of: a beautiful home, three wonderful boys, a good social life and a successful business. But there was an emptiness inside of me, something missing that I couldn't put my finger on.

I had joined a new Round Table group when it started in Ferndown and through that had a good circle of friends. One of them, Clive, described himself as a 'born-again Christian'. I thought he'd flipped. Helen was showing alarming religious tendencies too. Our 4-year-old, James, had been invited by his 'girlfriend' to a local Sunday school. One thing had led to another and Helen had found herself going more regularly to our local Anglican church, St Mary's Church, Ferndown.

Clive and his wife, Sue, were a sociable couple. Regularly they invited us to social occasions or meals at their home. There always seemed to be another Christian couple at these gatherings. We both enjoyed those evenings. For me, they were opportunities for a good debate, which I always enjoyed. Helen would rush back home and scour the Bible for flaws in their arguments. Through this time, something was stirring in me.

One night I asked Helen for her Rector's phone number.

When I called him, Revd Christopher Blissard-Barnes graciously invited me round to the Rectory. He sat on his high chair and I sat on the settee. I announced to him, 'I am a Jew, but I want to know about Jesus.' The look on his face was a picture of amazement and excitement. He calmly explained some basic facts including that Jesus Himself was also a Jew. At the end of our meeting he loaned me three books, *Basic Christianity* by John Stott, and two short tracts, *Journey Into Life* and *The Way Ahead.*

These things were helpful, but it was what he said to me as I was leaving that shook me.

'Ralph, have you ever read the New Testament?'

'Moi – a Jew? How ridiculous!' I thought. But one can't be rude to a stranger, so I simply said, 'No.'

He offered to visit me at our home and we booked an appointment for two or three weeks later.

Helen's Journey

In between my first and second meeting with Christopher, Helen had a profound experience of God at a Sunday 8.00am Book of Common Prayer communion service. Christopher was preaching on Revelation 3:20:

'Here I am! I stand at the door and knock. If anyone hears my voice and opens the door, I will go in and eat with him, and he with me.'

Christopher explained that Jesus waits to be invited into our lives and does not force His way in. Helen realised that she had never actually done that. Was that what had happened to Clive and Sue? For quite some time she had been envious of the way they seemed to know God personally. But, if she invited Jesus in, what might He require of her? It was a scary moment, but by now Helen was really hungry to know God. She silently asked Jesus to come in, but to lead her gently, one step at a time. Helen found her face wet with tears. She could not explain why she was crying. She was not unhappy, in fact quite the opposite. Now she realises that it was the Holy Spirit resting on her. At the time, she was more concerned about how to dodge the vicar in the hand-shaking queue on the way out, as she couldn't understand what had happened and she certainly didn't want to talk about it.

Kesher ('Connection') and Finding the Truth, YHWH Jesus

When Christopher came to our home it was three weeks after my visit, and two weeks after Helen invited Jesus into her life. We had a good debate discussing the books he had lent me. I felt I was winning the debate until he asked that same question again: *had I read the New Testament yet?* How about starting with what he considered to be the most Jewish Gospel, Matthew?

Then he suddenly asked, 'May I pray for you?' Now I *knew* what was coming, and I waited for the book of prayers to come out – the Christian version of the Jewish *Siddur*, I supposed. But to my astonishment this vicar just launched out in his own words. He put his hands together and simply prayed something like this: 'God, this man is searching for you. Will you reveal yourself to him? Amen.'

Wow! It was just as if Christopher had telephoned God saying, 'Hi God, this man Ralph is searching for you, will you reveal yourself to him?' It was the very *idea* of that kind of relationship with God that made me read all of the Gospel of Matthew. Hooked, I went on to read the other three gospels as well. I was completely taken aback!

The New Testament was a *Jewish* book, written by *Jewish* people, about *Jewish* people who fulfilled all the *Jewish* feasts and traditions. I started to wonder, 'Could Jesus be the long awaited Jewish Messiah?' It was mind-blowing!

Through all my reading there was one doubt that persisted in my mind. Is Jesus alive today? Or to put it another way, is he *YHWH*, the *Divine I Am*? That was what it all boiled down to. If He was divine, then from all I had read He was indeed the Messiah. If He wasn't, then I should steer clear of the vicar and Christianity. To resolve this for myself, I set God a challenge: could He send maybe six, or at least one person, to say to me, 'Jesus is Alive?'

That Sunday a curious compulsion took hold of me – to go with Helen to St Mary's morning service. That Sunday was the monthly family service. The boys were regularly attending the Sunday school now, so for the first time we went together as a whole family. The new guitar-singing curate Revd Bill Salmon had decided to teach the congregation a new, very repetitive chorus song. I sat in the pew, spellbound, while the other 200 people in the congregation joined together singing:

'Jesus is alive today,
Jesus is alive today,
Jesus is alive, very much alive,
Jesus is alive today.'

God had answered the request of a little Jewish boy.

October 1980 was the start of a journey from which I've never looked back and have never regretted. We used to sing a song, 'It's an Adventure Following Jesus'. That's just how it has felt: an adventure planned by God to the last detail. What has struck me all along is the way in which the Lord has led Helen and me, one step at a time. He's never shown us the whole picture, just revealed it slowly, slowly – or as we say in Italian, '*piano, piano...*'

A year later, at 36, I was baptised at St Mary's, Ferndown. It sealed what had already happened in my heart. Although it was an important sign for me to publicly declare to others my new-found faith, I don't believe that there is anything magic in the water. If I had died during that intervening year, I am sure that Jesus would have welcomed me into His Kingdom just the same. After all, God looks into our hearts, not on what we do on the outside.

Calling to the Gentiles

A couple of years after I became a Christian I was at a conference at the Bournemouth International Centre. During the worship the man next to me turned to me and asked in French, 'Do you speak French?' He'd picked the right person! We fell into a long conversation (and even ended up speaking Arabic with a touch of Hebrew!) It turned out that he was a rabbi who had been thrown out of his synagogue in Israel because he had met with Jesus while reading the New Testament. We invited him to come for a meal. He told me that he still kept total Kosher (the strict Jewish food laws). I said we could manage that and buy in Kosher food to be eaten off plastic plates.

As we ate together, I asked him why he still kept Kosher. After all, in Peter's vision God pronounced that no food is unclean (Acts 10:1-15). His answer made a deep impression on me: 'Ralph, like Paul you might be called to reach gentile Christians. But like Peter, my calling is to Jews. My house must be ritually clean so that orthodox Jews can come there.'

At around the same time I met a Jewish Christian whose pastor had asked him, at his baptism, to eat a ham sandwich to prove his total conversion. These two encounters helped me to see where my own Jewishness fits into my Christian faith. It's somewhere in the middle, between those two extremes. Although I believe that we're saved by grace and not by obedience to the Law, I believe we can enrich our understanding of the Christian faith and understand where Jesus was coming from as we look at our Jewish roots and traditions. You can read more about the Jewish feasts from a Christian perspective in the addendum at the end of this book.

Soon after I became a Christian I wrote to my mum to tell her. She replied (hoping to dismiss my new-found faith), 'Once you have been circumcised as a Jew, you are always a Jew.' And she was right. I *am* forever a Jew. My circumcision (*milah*) at eight days old was an outward sign of my belonging to the Covenant and a promise that if I obey the Law I shall be saved. But for me now, my salvation depends on something else – what Jesus Christ has done for me on the cross. By grace (not law) am I saved.

One of the Talmudic stories in my grandfather's book is about a 'Camel boy' who never forgets his roots.

'The story tells of a camel boy in the desert finding a man nearly dying of thirst. Having given him a drink, he offered to take him on his camel. The man turned out to be a king and took in the boy, educated and cared for him. In time, the boy was so favoured that he was made Prime Minister. The other ministers were so jealous that they wanted to get rid of him. They told the King that the camel boy was stealing from him and locked all he stole in a room that no one was allowed to enter. The King visited the camel boy and demanded to see the room. When the room was opened, the king was confused and could see nothing in the room except for some old ragged camel boy's outfits, which were just visible. When the King asked what was so special about these rags the boy replied, "I don't want to ever forget where I have come from and what you have given me.'"

Like that camel boy, I don't ever want to forget where I have come from, my Jewishness, or to lose sight of what Jesus has done for me.

Others Seeing the Connection

Gentiles often struggle to comprehend how I can still be Jewish, now that I am a Church of England clergyman. I reply with a simple question, 'What religion was Jesus?' It is great watching people's faces as the penny drops and they make the connection, in a fresh way, between the God of the Old and New Testament and the seamless story of God's plans and purposes told from Genesis to Revelation. Our faith is rooted in Jesus the Jewish Rabbi, who fulfilled all the Jewish law and kept all the Jewish feasts, because He was a Jew.

I remember one encounter I had on a French family holiday, soon after I'd become a Christian. A man we'd got chatting to over a drink one evening had gradually picked up the bare bones of my strange background.

'Let's get this straight', he said, congratulating himself on having disentangled it. 'You grew up in a Moslem country in a Jewish family and went to a Catholic school. I suppose you'll be telling me next', he added with a laugh, 'that you're a member of the Church of England!' My answer was quite simply, 'Yes!'

For the rest of that holiday he kept coming over to our caravan and looking at Helen and I with wonder, as if to say, 'Really?' We just nodded.

My Father Accepting My Faith

I can still feel the frustration I had that my father failed to react when I first told him I had become a Christian. After saying it twice more, each time in a different way, I felt the Lord telling me, 'Shut up!' It became obvious that he didn't want to discuss what I had done. 'But I need to know that he's heard me,' I argued with God. The Lord made me wait four months, until the time when Dad was making plans to visit my older brother in Atlanta. He phoned me and said, 'I'm coming back sooner, because our *Pessach* (Jewish Passover) is earlier than your Easter.' At that moment it was confirmed that he *had* heard me and we didn't need to discuss it any more – that would have only caused him more hurt.

The continuation of Israel (the Jewish people) is seen as depending on every Jew following Jewish tradition. The Talmud pulls no punches:

In a boat at sea, one of the men began to bore a hole in the bottom of the boat. On being remonstrated with, he answered: "I am only boring under my own seat." "Yes," said his comrades, "but when the sea rushes in we shall be drowned with you." So it is with Israel.'

In my father's eyes, I had not only betrayed him, but every Jewish person. I had become a *goy* – unclean – a gross insult on the lips of a Jewish person. I'm relieved to say that my father's response didn't involve him tearing his garments or declaring me dead, as one of my uncles did with one of his sons. Sadly, I was not able to include him in my spiritual journey. Often our conversations were stilted, because we had to avoid all reference to our church and our faith – a growing feature of our lives and my exciting journey of faith.

Christopher and Bill, the two ministers who had helped

us discover Jesus, were both instrumental in our growth as disciples of Jesus. Bill ran the confirmation classes which helped answer my many questions. There was a small group of us, but we enjoyed our time together and I felt we all grew in our spiritual journey.

One day, Bill asked Helen and I if we would offer our home to host a midweek fellowship group. We readily agreed and enjoyed welcoming around ten others at various stages of life and Christian maturity on a weekly basis. Bill led us for the first term, and we picked up a lot from him, not only spiritually, but also about how to manage group dynamics and discussions. At the end of the first term, Bill announced that he wasn't coming again, but was passing the leadership on to us. We were dropped in at the deep end, but quickly learned that when we step out in our weakness, God supplies His strength.

We were both encouraged to help with the children's groups on a Sunday morning. I helped and subsequently led one of the Pathfinder groups for 11-14 year olds. Helen led a group of 10-11's. Helen is certain she learned more than the children as she conscientiously prepared for each session. She was also involved with a ladies group and saw many come to the Lord.

We were growing fast in other ways too, receiving the baptism of the Holy Spirit and learning how to operate in the spiritual gifts of healing and prophecy. Christopher recognised God was calling me into leadership and invited me to take on the responsibility of churchwarden.

This was indeed a period of exciting adventure in a church where many were on the same journey under Christopher's wise and gentle leadership, always stretching and encouraging us forward.

Chapter 6
Call to Ordination

Journey Towards Ordination

A vocation, they say, is like toothache – if it's real, it keeps coming back. When I had the first inkling, after just three years as a Christian, that God might be calling me to ordination, Christopher, our Rector, said he thought it was too soon to be sure. 'Test it out for a while,' he said. That was the year that he promptly asked me to be churchwarden of St Mary's Church, instead. As I prayed about this totally unexpected invitation, it felt right that I should accept. In fact, I see my five years as churchwarden and the experience I gained, as part of my journey towards ordination.

The call came again while we were away at Lee Abbey, a Christian Conference Centre in Devon. I shared what I sensed God was saying to me with Helen as we enjoyed a long walk in the grounds with their spectacular views of the coast. God was reaffirming the call, but I felt God saying again, 'Not yet.' It was as if He was preparing me to get used to the idea, so that I would be ready to respond when the right time came.

Another year went by. By January 1987 a few changes had taken place in our family life. The previous April, James had moved to Monkton Combe School, a Christian boarding school near Bath. Olly joined him there in September 1987 and both of them responded well to the caring atmosphere and overt Christian witness. Mark had also left home to continue his studies up north in Bradford.

Then, just before Christmas, Helen's mother passed into a coma. Over a number of years she had been deteriorating with Parkinson's disease. All three boys were home for the Christmas vacation and were able to spend time with her to make their 'goodbyes'. On New Year's Eve she peacefully slipped away.

A few weeks later, while Helen was away on a conference, I was swimming my daily 100 lengths in our own indoor swimming pool when it hit me. It suddenly became clear that the time had come. And then the cost gripped me. We had so many luxuries we'd have to part with. Returning home I waited for Helen before I announced, 'I've got bad news for you: God is saying now is the time to offer for ordination.'

This time the call was here to stay and I knew that now was the time. With the younger two boys at Monkton, Mark in Bradford, and Helen's mother now gone, it was as if God had freed us up to be on the move with Him.

We broke the news to the boys with mixed reactions!

'Dad, you are totally over the top,' Mark said. 'But it's your life, you can throw it away if you want to.'

James immediately mentally counted the cost.

'I suppose it means we'll have to sell the house. But if that is what God is saying, it's okay by me.'

Olly had just sat through one of my sermons.

'I can see you as a vicar, Dad, but I can't see many people coming to your church.'

When news reached my Round Table friend Clive, who was by now ordained himself, the reaction was less muted: 'What took you so long?'

Full or Part-time Ordination?

I was faced with two choices, though. First, I needed to train. Would that be as a full-time student, giving up everything and moving away from Bournemouth? Or should I study at Salisbury during evenings and weekends, staying at work during the week? Even beyond that, the future was not cut and dried. Again it was a choice between full-time or part-time 'vicarhood'.

'What's it to be, then?' was Helen's immediate question when I arrived back from a vocational weekend at Bristol. Only one thing had become clear: whether full-time or part-time, the choice would apply to both my training and the work beyond. If it was to be full-time studies, then I felt it would be in Trinity College, Bristol.

It was the old Start-Rite shoe advert that settled it for us. God had given Helen the vision. In her mind's eye, she saw the two children happily walking along holding hands, the little boy wearing his satchel. They came to a crossroads where Jesus stood, one direction marked Salisbury and the other Bristol. The Salisbury route was brightly lit, the other less easy to see ahead. If they chose the Salisbury road, Jesus blessed them, but remained at the crossroads which was also the cross. On the other hand, when Helen watched them taking the Bristol route instead, the boy left his satchel at the foot of the cross, but Jesus walked between them holding each of them by the hand.

As we prayed through the choices that Jesus had laid before us, we both instinctively knew which way to choose. We decided that we'd rather walk anywhere holding Jesus' hands, even if the way ahead was not fully visible. This vision proved to be very significant on our journey, returning to reassure us in times of doubt or difficulty.

The next few months were filled with interviews of various kinds, as several members of the Church of England tested out my calling. This culminated in an official selection conference at the end of November that year: an intensive three days of interviews and small group activities with other candidates. Several days afterwards the telephone rang at 8 o'clock in the morning. I picked up the receiver to hear the bishop offering me congratulations: I had been selected to go forward for training.

In preparation for a possible move to Bristol and theological college, we had begun to investigate housing in the area. There was very little on the market, but we were keeping in touch with a new development in Hanham, on the east side of the city. It was within easy distance of the college and for travelling to Bath to visit James and Olly at school. A couple of days after the bishop phoned me, we heard the good news that a plot we particularly liked had unexpectedly become available. We put down a token deposit. The house would be completed at the end of May. Then, to our amazement, some Round Table friends made us an excellent offer on our home in Ferndown. Doors were continuing to open before us. God's timing became perfect when the completion of the sale of our friends' house tied in exactly with the completion of our newly built Bristol home. God had taken care of all the details.

Telling My Parents

The next hurdle was to break the news to my parents. It was going to take a lot of courage and wisdom. I was right to be anxious. That was the beginning of seven years of restricted and strained contact with my father. Only God's grace sustained me through this relational turmoil and, as mentioned earlier, only

God's intervention would restore the relationship in later years.

Shortly afterwards we grasped the nettle and went to visit Mum in Miami. Right at the beginning of our visit I dropped the bombshell that I would be entering the Anglican ministry. As the daughter of a rabbi, Mum needed time to digest and reflect on what she had heard. She consulted the rest of the family, and especially her brothers, Edmond and Eliaho.

When we were alone, a few days later, she told me that she'd 'been thinking'. She said that Uncle Edmond didn't agree, but Uncle Eliaho had said it was up to her to pray it through. She went on to tell me, 'I can't understand it, but I believe that God is calling you. I even want to bless you.' I was completely blown away – it came right out of the blue! It was so surreal I began to wonder if I'd dreamt it. But just before we left to fly home, Mum took Helen on one side and told her that she felt God had called me. 'I want you to know Ralph has my blessing,' she said. 'God loves all people.'

Another major consideration concerned the future of our two optical practices. Bernard Perry had joined me first as an employee and, in time, as a partner. It was now agreed that for the time being I would become a 'sleeping partner', with a view to selling out completely to Bernard at a later date.

With God's help we had tied up all the loose ends and moved to Hanham at the end of May. Helen was there full time, putting the house in order, and I stayed with friends Monday to Friday, continuing to work in the practice until the end of July.

Theological College

Bristol it was, then. The Principal, George Carey, had interviewed me at Trinity College, but left as soon as I accepted the place to become the Bishop of Bath and Wells and subsequently the Archbishop of Canterbury.

In September 1988 I started the 2-year course which would turn me from a Messianic Jew into a Messianic Jewish Vicar. Theological college was not quite what I'd hoped for. I was expecting the opportunity to really dig into the Bible, with deep theological discussions and debates. The reality was more like skating across the surface of Scripture at high speed. However, looking back it was a good foundation for ministry.

It was a long time since I had written any essays, so this was something of a challenge. God also used this as a time of refining and testing for both Helen and me. This was not always comfortable, but looking back, a vital part of the training. We both valued the fellowship and friendship of others on the journey towards ordination and the midweek worship sessions in which spouses were encouraged to participate. There was a rich variety of style and experimentation was encouraged; and there was always an amazing sense of the presence of God. This was a time of rapid growth for both of us.

At the end of my first year, I was invited to consider the position of curate back in Bournemouth, at St. Andrew's, Kinson. The Revd Vic Barron had recently become the Rector and I was to join him a year later in the summer of 1990, after completing my studies at Trinity.

In Spring 1990 I got the wobbles. They hit me just 3 months before I was due to be ordained. Suddenly, I really wasn't sure I was 'good enough' to go forward for ordination. It was a horrible feeling. For me it had to be 100% or nothing – I can't work any other way. So I wrote to my tutor, Revd Peter Williams, telling him that I was seriously considering not going ahead with ordination. We had sacrificed so much to get to this point, but did I have what it takes to fulfil this calling?

The following day I left with a student team from Trinity on a week of mission to St Mary's Church, Longfleet, Poole. It was being led by our Principal, David Gillett. That was how I came to be staying at the home of our old Bournemouth friends Ray Fardon, a retired, ordained head-teacher, and his wife, Pam. We had initially met them at Lee Abbey in Devon and they had previously encouraged us to step out in faith by taking us out with mission teams to Weston-Super-Mare and the Isle of Wight. On this occasion, I found myself caught up in a whirl of activity, going from home to home, leading groups as the week went on. Busy in ministry, I said nothing to the team about what I was feeling.

On the Wednesday evening, 28th March 1990, I was asked to lead a meeting at Ray and Pam's house. At the end of the meeting I suggested we pray for each other. Everyone was prayed for, but no one prayed for me. I could barely suppress the niggling doubts about my future, and I felt the Lord saying that I should ask for prayer, so I mumbled something like, 'Could you could pray for me as I am due to lead tomorrow's evening service?' With that simple request God took over.

Is it Tongues or Arabic?

Ray stood up and spoke out, 'No. We must all lay hands on you and pray now, because God has something to say to you.' Ray started to pray in what he presumed to be tongues. I heard something else coming out of his mouth. It was the familiar Sudanese Arabic of my childhood, as clear as day:

'Allah be'hebak – Inta min al dam beta Ibrahiem – Al Angiel fi fomak.'

'God loves you,' Ray was speaking in a language totally alien to him. 'You are from the blood of Abraham. The Gospel is in your mouth.' I was the only person in the room who understood. Then Ray added in English, 'You are to proclaim the Gospel and bring my people to the Kingdom.'

Then total silence. Wow! By then I was totally on the floor.

After that came more words of encouragement – in English this time – spoken by Pam from God for me:

'The battle is not yours but mine. You are not to doubt your ministry. Minister in my name and proclaim the Gospel.' She added, 'Breath in His love, strength and courage. Do not be afraid. I am with you always. Many will be brought into the Kingdom by you. GO and proclaim the Gospel and minister in my name.'

God even gave me a hug, lovingly administered by one of the other Trinity students. Then, of course, I had to explain all about the doubts I'd been having.

I was completely overwhelmed. Early the next morning I met Peter Hunter, who was also part of the team. Peter and I shared a study in Trinity and he was my prayer partner. He was the only other person to whom I had confided my anxieties earlier that week. I had to be sure that he had said nothing to anyone. He assured me that he was still the only person who knew anything about it. Now the whole exciting story of the previous evening bubbled out.

Meanwhile, back in Bristol, Helen was very concerned. She'd had a call from my tutor saying that of course I shouldn't give up and could he see me as soon as I got back? As Helen prayed for me, she was reassured by remembering the Start-Rite picture. It seems that God had given that picture for crisis moments of doubt such as this. Helen prayed fervently that I would know God's affirmation of His call on my life.

When Helen told me of my tutor's concern I told her not

to worry, God had spoken to me in Arabic to proceed with my ordination. I sometimes wonder why God intervened with such a miracle to confirm my call. I am so thankful that He did. From that day I never looked back. I had an unshakable confidence that it was God who had called me to this work, and that was enough.

Ordination and Curate in Kinson

So, by the amazing grace of God, I was ordained in Salisbury Cathedral on 30th June 1990. The pre-ordination retreat was an extraordinary affair. It turned out that the silent retreat house was not quite big enough to accommodate all the ordinands. Two of us had to be farmed out to a rather sumptuous flat in one of the nearby houses in the Close. Peter Gibbs and I, total strangers then, ended up together there for the simple reason that our surnames came consecutively on the list. We forged a strong friendship during that retreat that continues to this day and we often reminisce about our first encounter. God always knows what He is doing.

'I think we were both in a state of shock,' remembers Peter. 'We felt like fish out of water in this museum-like place filled with precious antiques. Neither of us knew the protocol. So we wrestled first with the idea of breaking the silence, then about taking ourselves off to the pub for some solace.' It was over a pint that we discovered that we were destined for neighbouring parishes in Dorset – not the place either of us had trained for ordination. There were more God-incidences. First, I was going as curate to Kinson, a place Peter knew well – he'd spent part of his teens living there – and Peter was going as curate to the very church in Ferndown where I had met the Lord for the first time, St Mary's Church.

Peter and Jane have remained good friends and prayer partners with Helen and I ever since. We still meet regularly to encourage and support each other.

So a major shift of emphasis came about in my life. Instead of being involved with people's physical sight, I would be dealing with their spiritual problems. Thinking it over since, I've begun to see the parallels:

To the short-sighted I try to bring spiritual sight.
For the long-sighted I aim to help them to see close detail.
For those with astigmatism, I hope to make their distorted vision come clear.
Just as in my practice, I help to remove barriers to vision such as sending them to have their cataracts removed and to heal damaged retinas which prevent clear vision of the truth.

In each of the four churches I was privileged to minister in, I saw God's hand at work building His kingdom.

Chapter 7
Curate at St Andrew's Church, Kinson

Joining the Kinson Team

St Andrew's Church, Kinson (Bournemouth) gave me the chance to get to grips with all that is involved in being an ordained minister. There were actually two churches involved in the team, and I was based at the parent church, working under the direction of the team Rector, Vic Barron. Vic and his wife, Jill, did everything to make us feel at home and part of the team. Every Monday morning Vic, Richard (the team Vicar) and I would meet together to pray, plan and share pastoral issues. Our wives met up later in the morning to share and pray together and took it in turns to provide lunch, which we all shared together. Vic's example of including wives as part of the team was a model we valued.

The Lord blessed Helen and me by our coming to know Him at around the same time. As we've grown spiritually alongside each other, He's enabled us to use our complementary gifts together in ministry. This became apparent when we arrived in Kinson and we've worked together in many ways ever since. I'm good at getting people talking. Helen's good at hearing what they're not saying, reading between the lines. This has often enabled us to be effective in helping those we are counselling to open up to the Lord's healing power.

The team in Kinson also gave me plenty of experience in the occasional offices – baptisms, weddings and funerals. Being close to Bournemouth, it was a retirement area and between the three of us, (Vic, Richard and I) we conducted around 150 funerals each year. The parent church, St. Andrews, was a very attractive setting for weddings and most Saturdays in the summer months we would conduct two or three weddings.

Vic gradually released me into different ministries and responsibilities. An early one was to lead the youth group. We settled on Sunday afternoons for these meetings at our home. Twelve to fifteen 14-18 year olds piled into our open plan living room, occupying the sofa chairs and even the stairs! I am convinced they came to our youth group meetings mainly for Helen's chocolate cake, not my wonderful teaching, but it was a privilege to disciple such an enthusiastic bunch. After teaching, prayer and tea, we would walk *en masse* around the corner to St. Andrews Church for the evening service.

On Sunday mornings we enjoyed the worship and the friendly family atmosphere: I learned a lot from Vic about planning services and preaching. Vic was brilliant at family services. I will never forget the time he stood up at the front in his chef's hat to make a 'man'. He mixed together the required ingredients – 90% water, nails for iron etc. – then he asked the children why they thought it wasn't working!

At the main morning service, the church would be packed. People very rarely arrived late because they would not find a seat. Vic had already been thinking about planting a new congregation, and had invited me to join the team, partly because he sensed I had a heart for this. Or perhaps it was that, as an older curate (aged 45), he considered my maturity and business experience to be an asset in leading a team. We started to pray and plan. Then, 16 months after my ordination day, I found myself charged with the job of setting up a new congregation in a far corner of the parish.

Emmanuel Church

During Lent, the church members were asked to pray about whether they were being called to be a part of the new congregation. A team of 24 resulted. Several members of the youth group were ready to be part of this new adventure and we were delighted, seeing this as an opportunity to encourage them to discover and develop their God-given gifts. In fact, they ended up leading our Sunday worship. My Jewish heritage meant that I valued every generation as part of the family.

The oldest member of the team was Phyllis, a lady in her 80s. When she expressed a desire to be included, but wondered if she was too old to be part of the team, I said, 'Definitely not' – for I had already recognised that she was an intercessor. We enjoyed many prayer meetings led by Phyllis in her home. She made sure we got down to prayer promptly and then after an hour she would put the kettle on and make us all a hot drink. After 10 minutes or so, she would say, 'Well, my dears, I won't keep you any longer. I know you are all very busy.' That was our cue to go home!

We had our team, but we had nowhere to meet. At a parish away day, we were once more praying about this and considering possible alternatives. Suddenly someone said, 'What about the DDA building?' I didn't even know it existed, but felt very excited. On the way home, several of us went to find it, hidden away in a small field, surrounded by the back gardens of flats and houses. A narrow driveway gave access to it from the road. It was a slightly run down, prefabricated building, but of a good size. It belonged to the Disabled Drivers Association and, after making a couple of enquiries, it turned out that the Chairman of the committee was a builder who had worked on our house in Ferndown 15 years previously. The building was only used occasionally and they were happy to rent it to us for Sunday mornings. God had led us to the place he had chosen.

We called a meeting in the DDA building for all those interested. At that time we had an Archdeacon from South America visiting us and when he heard we were meeting to set up a church plant, he thought we needed to bring along trowels and bricks to start the building. Back home in Ecuador, that is how they planted new churches.

We set up an overhead projector and I asked all who were present to share ideas and suggestions regarding the church plant. Some were not workable. Others produced a ministry of their own. Someone asked about flowers. We decided we would have flowers each Sunday but, as the building was not in use during the week, we would give them away after the service to someone who was sick or in need of encouragement. This became a simple but much appreciated way for the church family to share the love of Jesus.

At that session the congregation's name was revealed as someone shared a Bible verse:

'This is how you will know that the living ***God is among you****, and that certainly he will drive out before you the [tribes in your way].'* (Joshua 3:10)

Emmanuel – God is with us. That was it! The name, once spoken, resonated with the whole gathering. Emmanuel church had been conceived and a starting date was set for 6th October.

Phyllis had a daughter, Liz, who lived in China. She taught English in a university, but her main reason for being in China was to share the Gospel. As she taught about the English cultural traditions of Christmas and Easter, students would come to her privately to ask about Jesus and several were baptised in the bath in her apartment.

That summer she had been flown home to England for surgery on her back. She had suffered an injury resulting in a herniated disc and was in so much pain that she spent much of the time laying flat on the floor. Every time anyone was willing to pray, she was ready to be prayed for. Several times we laid hands on her and anointed her with oil.

The date for surgery was set just before the inaugural service of Emmanuel. As the surgery date approached, Liz shared that the pain had subsided and she had reduced her dose of pain killers. On the day she was admitted to hospital, Phyllis and Helen were praying together in the afternoon. Suddenly the phone rang. When Phyllis answered, it was Liz asking Phyllis to send a taxi. Her operation had been cancelled. A pre-op X-ray (scans were rare in 1991), unlike the previous X-ray which revealed the herniated disc, revealed no abnormality. There was no longer any need for surgery. Liz was able to join us for the opening service, sharing her testimony and using dance to glorify God.

Liz's surgeon was astonished. He was so convinced that she would need surgery that he refused to let Liz return to China until she had had several check-ups and six months had passed. After six months he wrote to Liz saying, 'Much to my surprise it looks as if your previous abnormality has resolved itself.' We kept a copy of the letter to glorify God for His healing power. Liz's testimony and her gifts of mime and dance were an added bonus at Emmanuel in those early months.

So, Emmanuel Church was born. God was indeed with us. We saw the church grow from 24 to over 70 in the first year. At the opening service, 50 people arrived. Right from the beginning there was a special anointing on the worship, which ushered in a sweet presence of God. Our worship team consisted mainly of teenagers under 18 years old. As they approached their A-Level exams, an even younger team of 11-14 year-olds took over. Ali Dorey who played the flute became our main worship leader. She eventually trained for ordination herself. I still find myself praying for all those young people.

On Advent Sunday, several weeks after our first service, the Bishop came at Vic's suggestion to conduct an official opening service. Our dance group worshipped in dance to the song, 'Emmanuel, O Emmanuel, filled with awe we worship at your feet, and sing Emmanuel, God is with us….' The presence of God filled the building.

After receiving communion we all went out to the car park, as some of the parent church congregation joined us. We continued worshiping by singing, 'Shine Jesus, shine, fill this land with the Father's glory.' Those two songs summed up God's purpose for Emmanuel –intimate worship in the presence of God and the spreading of His glory to the community around.

During the time I led Emmanuel church I learnt the importance of leaning on God when decisions had to be made. I was still a curate and was learning rapidly on the job. God blessed me with a great team to help support me, especially my two churchwardens, John and Dennis. They were mature Christians and a wonderful support. As an added bonus, they were both excellent preachers and gifted in prophecy.

The Importance of Integrity

As Emmanuel grew in numbers we had more children coming. Next door, another smaller building stood, where cycling proficiency training was based. I noted it was not being used on Sundays and contacted the leader to see if we could use it for the children. He informed me there was a covenant restricting the building's use to cycling proficiency training only. He suggested we could call our children's group an extension of that work and so get around the covenant.

As I prayed, the Lord clearly showed me that this deception would not honour to Him. Not wanting to dishonour the Lord, I contacted the local council. After being passed from one department to another, I finally got through to the right person. He said it would be good to use the building and he gave us permission to use it on Sunday without charge, whilst lifting the covenant was investigated.

Six months later the cycling proficiency group closed down. Had we not honoured the Lord when we began, we would have no longer been able to use the building. Instead we had permission to continue and favour with the council. I learnt the importance of honesty and integrity. God can overcome all obstacles when we put our trust in Him!

I was greatly blessed to have Vic Barron as my mentor. I learnt a great deal from him. He was not only a great teacher and expositor of the Word but, together with his wife Jill, he was also a wonderful support to me and Helen. They both remained good friends as God called us on to our next assignment.

My grandfather, Chief Rabbi Solomon Malka (1878–1949)

My grandmother, Rubbisa Hanna Malka

Interior of the Khartoum synagogue

Interior of the Khartoum synagogue

Family holiday

Family holiday

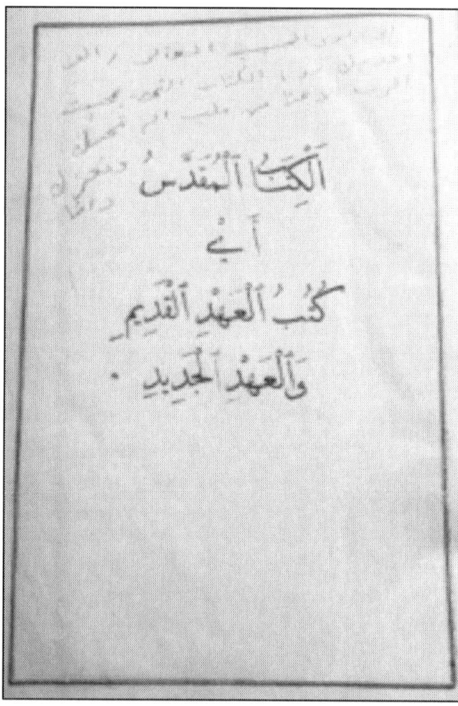

الكتاب المقدس
أي
كتب العهد القديم
والعهد الجديد

The Arabic Bible my mother gave me

Purim Party celebration. I am the cowboy, my brother Sol the Indian on the left, and my sister the beautiful Arab lady and cousins

At the back my two brothers, Adolph on my left, Sol on my right. In front, Mum, my sister Claudette and her daughter, Rachel in front

Comboni College, Khartoum

Comboni College, Khartoum

Fading frontage of Maurice Goldenberg's shop in Khartoum – the only proof that Jews once lived in Sudan

Our wedding day

Our family me and Helen and our three boys, Mark James and Olly

Our growing family with our seven grandchildren

Chapter 8
St Andrew's Church, Edgware

Messianic Jew in Edgware

Believe it or not, I am not the only Messianic Jew (a Jew who believes the Messiah Jesus has come) who's a clergyman in the UK. Revd John Fieldsend, another Messianic Jew, has been our friend for many years. We first met soon after I was ordained, when John came to St Andrew's Church, Kinson, as a representative of CMJ – the Churches' Ministry among Jewish People. We immediately warmed to each other and kept in contact. Through John I also developed an interest in CMJ and the work they do amongst Jewish populations around the world.

Fourteen months after worship started at Emmanuel Church, John phoned to tell me about a vacancy in the parish of Edgware, a very Jewish area in Northwest London. John wondered if I should consider applying. I hadn't been considering a move just yet, but as I prayed about it, it seemed right to apply.

At first the Rector, Colin Bedford, had reservations about considering my application, on the very grounds of my Jewishness, and laid my application to one side. He was afraid that it might close doors to Christian ministry in this Jewish area of London, especially as there had been one or two sensitive situations between the church and local synagogues, when Jews had expressed an interest in discovering who Jesus is.

Colin sent me a very nice letter explaining that I hadn't been short listed and wishing me well for the future. Although, on the face of it, that was the end of the matter, and we hadn't been anticipating a move, our hearts had warmed towards Edgware. Helen even expressed the feeling that the door had not shut and that she wouldn't be surprised if another letter came. What a great prophetic wife I have. A month later, after the first round of interviews took place and no suitable candidate had been found, I had a phone call from Colin inviting me for an interview.

Colin and his wife, June, were a warm and welcoming couple who loved people and we loved them right from the start. Colin explained that there were three churches in the team: St. Margaret's, the parent church, was on the bustling high street; St. Philip's served a post-war high rise housing estate; and St. Andrews, where the vacancy had occurred, served an area of the parish clearly defined by both the A41 and the M1 motorway. There were several synagogues of differing traditions in the parish, one of which was in the St. Andrew's area. The interview day was very positive and it felt like God had brought us together with everyone we met. I was offered the vacancy and accepted.

Our parsonage in Edgware was in a cul-de-sac just behind the church, which had the very appropriate Old Testament name of Beulah Close. Beulah is the Hebrew word for 'marriage', as in Isaiah 62:4b: *'But you will be called Hephzibah, and your land Beulah; for the Lord will take delight in you, and your land will be married.'* There were 22 houses in the close, 19 of which were occupied by Jewish families. Curtains twitched in the close at the arrival of the Jewish Vicar.

One day, as Helen wrestled with the weeds in the overgrown front garden, a neighbour opposite came across for a chat. He had obviously been chewing over the confusion of having a Messianic Jew as a neighbour. He said, 'Ralph's still quite Jewish, isn't he? He seems to have a foot in both camps.' Helen took the opportunity to explain that I am still Jewish, but had come to know Jesus as my Messiah. St Paul didn't say he wasn't a Jew now that he was a follower of Christ, he declared *'I am a Jew…'* (Acts 21:39)

A different neighbour was also puzzled. She asked Helen, 'If Ralph wanted to become more religious, why didn't he become a Rabbi?' Her remark gave Helen another opportunity to share my testimony. A Jewish Anglican clergyman provokes all sorts of reactions, not all of them positive. Indeed, some can be quite hostile.

At my first local group meeting of CCJ (Council of Christians and Jews), that seeks to promote understanding between Christians and Jews, I was having a conversation with one of the local Rabbis. One of our neighbours joined us saying, 'Oh, Rabbi, this is the new Jewish Vicar I was telling you about.' The Rabbi ended the conversation abruptly. From that time forward he was no more than coldly polite if ever we met.

On another occasion we held an open evening at the church with Jewish food and Israeli dancing. We had given an invitation to the whole community. A lot of people came. Two members of the local Lubavich Synagogue stood outside St Andrew's Church handing out leaflets, giving a public warning to Jews against going to a Messianic Jewish Church.

It was during our time at Edgware that I became even more aware of the profound importance of my Jewish roots and the richness that the knowledge of these brings to Christian worship and understanding. With the encouragement of contacts from CMJ, and with both Jews and Gentiles wanting to learn more, I started a Saturday morning Messianic fellowship which we called Beit Yeshua (the house of Jesus). We also occasionally invited people to our house on a Friday evening to experience a Sabbath meal, preceded by the traditional liturgy prayers of blessing for all family members.

On one of these occasions, we invited a young mum who regularly attended the church's toddler group. She had been brought up as a Jew, but had abandoned her faith and lived with the gentile father of her four children. As I conducted the familiar proceedings she started to cry and couldn't stop. 'It's just like my granddad used to do it!' she said. We were grateful we had been able to reconnect her with her heritage.

Clearing the Church

During one of my early sermons I told a little story (all Jews love their little stories):

'A Jewish woman came to her rabbi with an offer she thought he couldn't refuse. She had replaced her 20-year old lounge suite with a new one and she'd decided to donate the old one to the synagogue. The wary rabbi asked her gently if it might not be wiser to sell the suite and give the *money* to the synagogue instead. "Oh, I've tried to sell it," she replied, horrified. "But I was told it is not worth anything!"'

It is a story that challenges us all. Do we give our best to God, or our castoffs?

As I was already discovering, that story is typical of how people react in the Christian Church, too. A store room in the church was full of junk, including four broken cookers and a large number of woodworm-infected chairs, so we proposed a Saturday morning clear out. When I suggested this, I was told it had been done not so long ago, but nevertheless we went ahead. On the appointed day, the question Helen and I kept asking was, 'When was the last time you used this item?' All the items that were not needed were put out on the lawn. It had been arranged for a man with a removal van to collect all that we put out. We filled the van!

Edgware Team

My experience of working in a team with Vic had been excellent and the team in Edgware was just as enjoyable. We had a wonderful team under Colin's capable, experienced leadership. Our staff meeting always started with a Bible reading and discussion of God's Word. His wife, June, heard so much laughter coming out of Colin's study that she wondered if we ever did any work.

Colin had a photographic memory. I remember being astounded at how much he managed to retain of a book which he'd only scanned his eyes over at breakneck speed. He loved books and ran a thriving bookshop out of the vicarage. I soon became aware that he had an impressive circle of friends and acquaintances, that he'd built up over his lifetime. It became a standing joke in the team that whoever we mentioned, Colin had met, or he'd stayed in the room next door to them at some time. Colin was very much a releasing, supportive and encouraging leader. I remember once, during St. Andrews refurbishment, when I was anxious about meeting an unexpected bill. He came to see me to let me know that St Margaret's Church PCC were fully behind our project and had decided to support us financially. What generosity.

We took weddings in turn between the three clergy: Colin, me, and John at St. Philip's. A couple requested to have their wedding on a Saturday when it was my turn to officiate. When they heard that my name was Goldenberg, they refused to have me officiate at their wedding. Colin stepped in and used his diplomatic skills to diffuse the situation. He made it clear that they could only be married by me, as he fully supported my Christian faith. I was truly grateful to be in a team that supported me and appreciated my Jewish roots.

Refurbishing the Church – God Provides

The church had been built in the late 1930s by John Laing, who was building the houses on the estate, but it had hardly been touched since. The heating didn't work properly, the electricity was a death-trap, and its flat roofs were leaking constantly. We felt the physical state of the building reflected the spiritual state of the church. This is especially important in a Jewish community: if a Jew sees a house falling into disrepair, he assumes that God is not blessing that place.

So, a major building project was called for. In addition, we felt we needed an upper room to be added at the back of the church for the youth and children's work, if possible. Big money was needed. It was evident that the project could be just about as big as the money we could throw at it. We thought we would need at least £100k to do all of the work, but how could that amount be raised by a small congregation? 'It will take a miracle.' I thought. By now I should have known that God loves to do miracles.

As we prayed, the church council and I felt the Lord was guiding us to multiply by four times whatever we raised through Lent running up to Easter Sunday, and put that amount of refurbishment work in hand, by faith. I was told that previous gift days had usually raised about £3,000. This multiplied by 4 would result in £12,000, which would have just about paid for the central heating which was on its last legs. The sum of £25,000, we were hoping for, was a huge amount in 1995. Gifts and prayer for the project were invited from the small congregation of around 50 at the time during Lent. And the miracles started happening.

One day a lady of pretty humble means came to me and asked a question. How much, she wanted to know, did she need to give extra each week in order to produce the necessary £25k over a 4-year covenant? I did some quick calculations: 25k divided by the 50 members of the congregation equalled £500, which when divided by 4 years gave £125 per annum or the surprising figure of £2.50 per week, less the tax relief! 'In that case,' she said, 'I will give a fiver extra a week.'

On Easter Sunday, like everyone else, I waited in eager anticipation to hear what had been given or promised. The treasurer announced the staggering sum of over £24,800, and someone immediately came to me offering to bridge the £200 gap needed to reach our £25,000 target! This meant that we could put in hand all the work we intended to do. God is good and faithful.

It was a great exercise in faith as we watched God supply our financial needs, often to the last penny and at the last minute. By the time we left Edgware, the church had a smart, newly refurbished building in which to praise God and thank Him for His abundant generosity. Moreover, we'd completely paid all the money, over £120,000, which included some extras that we hadn't even dreamt would be possible. God had supernaturally provided all that was needed for the task.

One day, I was sat at my desk opening the post. As I opened the first letter it contained a bill for £5,000. At that time we did not have any extra money to spare in the church funds. As I considered this, I picked up the next letter and opened it. Inside there was a cheque from a Building Society for exactly £5,000. When I phoned the Building Society to enquire who it was from so that I could thank them, I was told they could not tell me. To this day I do not know who sent it, but thank God for stirring that person to send us that exact sum to pay the bill.

Kingdom Connections

The summer after I arrived at St Andrew's we went to New Wine with some members of the church. We had heard about this summer camping week, with its emphasis on Charismatic worship and inspiring talks and workshops for both leaders and church members, and were excited to hear it was on the church calendar. The summer conferences were run by David Pytches and his church, another St. Andrews, in Chorleywood.

My abiding memory of that week was witnessing or being engulfed in laughter. An outpouring of the Holy Spirit in the Toronto Airport Vineyard Church a few months earlier had made its way across the Atlantic. Church leaders had gone to witness the extraordinary outpouring of God's love, accompanied by many strange manifestations, and it had followed them home.

We had already been over to Chorleywood for some leaders training days, and had also been to one of their 10-day retreats for clergy and their spouses, six months into our time at St. Andrews.

The retreat was run in the home of retired clergyman Teddy and his wife, Margaret. We were mightily blessed during the week. We were led in worship by a very young Matt Redman and teaching sessions were led by members of the staff team, including Barry Kissel and David Pytches, as well as visiting leaders from other Charismatic churches. These leaders shared their stories of church growth and prayed for us using spiritual gifts including prophecy.

During that retreat we visited John Coles in St. Barnabas, Finchley, and were inspired by his story of how God had used him to grow a small traditional congregation into a vibrant Spirit-filled church. The whole retreat was an amazing time of being saturated in the Holy Spirit and learning to walk in the power of the Spirit. I remember David Pytches praying over me that I had an Apostolic calling. Bruce Collins also prophesied over us and, to Helen's amazement, sensed that she would grow in the gifts of preaching and prophecy.

Back at St. Andrews we were noticing an increase in the tangible presence of the Holy Spirit. People were visibly affected as we prayed for them and faith levels were rising. A few months later, we were at Chorleywood for a day conference and in the afternoon David Pytches shared about his recent visit to the church in Toronto. David invited people who were feeling the presence of God to come forward for prayer. Helen shot to the front and the next moment my reserved wife was rolling around the floor, helpless with laughter. By way of further embarrassment David looked at me and said, 'Is your wife normally like this?' Then he announced to everyone, 'She's a vicar's wife you know!' Yes, we were mightily blessed by St Andrew's Chorleywood and New Wine.

Following that summer John Coles invited a few local church leaders to join him on a regular basis to pray and support each other. John had been encouraging us since we had met him during the retreat. He had a vision to run large events locally. Paul Sands, a Free Church minister who I already knew through the local ecumenical renewal group (coincidentally called Beulah) and I joined him. Before we knew it, we were involved in a conference organised in the large sports hall of Inglis Barracks, Mill Hill, a local Army place. Marc Dupont was the main speaker. He has a strong prophetic gifting and is regularly used by God to anoint others with the power of the Holy Spirit. John Coles continues to be a blessing to many church leaders and the mantle of leadership for the New Wine movement was passed on to him by David Pytches on his retirement.

Our time in Edgware was full of many extraordinary experiences and adventures in faith, but our stay there was not to be forever. The Lord had an important learning experience waiting for me.

Chapter 9
Christ Church, Harrow

Going to Harrow

I saw the Team Vicar position at Christ Church, Roxeth, Harrow, advertised and somebody suggested I apply for the position. I met with the Rector, Bruce Collins, who had prophesied over us on the Hensol retreat. He was very gifted in prophetic ministry and as a result was becoming much in demand as a speaker at conferences to teach and encourage others in the gift of prophecy – to the extent that he was absent from the parish much of the time and needed to hand on the leadership of Christ Church. At the interview, I asked how much freedom I would be given in leading the church. I understood I was to have total freedom. Having experienced such freedom and support in both Kinson and Edgware, I assumed the team in Harrow would be the same.

Prayer is an amazing resource! Whenever I am confronted by a big decision I ask my close Christian friends to help me pray it through. Sometimes everything becomes clear. But this time was not so clear – the responses from those I asked to pray came back very mixed. However, after meeting Bruce I felt it was right to accept the position when it was offered to me.

There was a great team of lay people in the church. They were full of wisdom, incredible gifts and a lot of experience. I was looking forward to working with them. Little did I know the challenges that would lie ahead.

Even before we arrived, we became aware of an issue that needed to be addressed. Six months earlier, the times of all the services had been changed. There had been a good reason behind this decision. The evening service was suspended for a time, as J.John was speaking on Sunday evenings in the area and the local churches were meeting together to support these mission meetings. In anticipation of new Christians, a new morning service called 'Open Doors' was introduced at 11.15am, with the knock-on effect of combining the two existing services into an earlier one. As a concession, an early 8.00am service was added once a month.

As a result, many people were unhappy and disgruntled about the loss of 'their' service when I arrived. In particular, the combined morning service, which was trying to blend two very different worship styles, needed a lot of time and energy to settle matters. Not until later, when we reverted to a main service at 10.30am and twice a month at 8.30am were we able to find peace. It proved hard to maintain someone else's vision.

After a couple of years, Fran Caldecourt became our church administrator. She also became a close friend. Fran had been a senior hospital nurse and subsequently a senior administrator to the local health authority, but felt called to work for the church. She later trained for ordination and eventually became vicar of a church not far from Harrow. She was very gifted in administration, and alongside this she used her pastoral gifts. One day after lunch in the vicarage, as we reflected on church life together over her favourite brew of Early Grey tea, Fran aptly summed up the role of church leadership, saying, 'Running a church is like running a hospital ward, except you do not discharge any of the patients!'

Refurbishing the Church

Christ Church was situated half way down Harrow hill. It had been built in the Victorian era for the servants of the wealthy who worshipped at St. Marys on the top of the hill. The pews were very uncomfortable and it was time to refurbish the worship area. The pews were to be replaced with more comfortable seats and the unused choir stalls could be cleared from the chancel area. This would make space for our more modern expressions of worship and a full immersion baptistery to be fitted. Charlie, our architect, had a clear vision of how to refurbish the church with a semi-circular seating arrangement. Charlie gave a very clear initial presentation to the church which included how church buildings had changed down the centuries to adapt to changing lifestyles and cultures.

An attempt to bring change 10 years previously had failed and there was a mixed reaction. We took time to explain the need for change and Charlie drew up plans and an artist's impression of how the building could be updated, including the refurbishment of the church kitchens to meet current health and safety regulations. He negotiated with the DAC (Diocesan Advisory Committee) and sorted out builders and costs. At a further meeting samples of possible chairs were available for people to comment on. At that meeting, an 80-year-old lady shared that 10 years previously she had firmly rejected any change, but following my visit to her, explaining how versatile the building would be in reaching out to younger generations, she not only supported the change, but would buy the first chair. I have to confess I felt quite tearful, in a positive way, and was glad when Clive took over leading the meeting. The meeting fully supported the plans.

We then faced another struggle with the Victoria Society,

English Heritage and the DAC to grant us permission to proceed with the project. However, after various meetings, and minor compromises on our part, the objections were overcome and the necessary permissions were granted.

Fran managed and organised the practical details of moving furniture and organising builders. John Price dealt with all the finances and negotiations with Charlie and the builder.

The refurbishment cost over a quarter of a million pounds, but transformed our worship area into a more versatile space. We were able to use the area for a variety of events, including 'Passover meals' which I led with seating for over 100 people. The full immersion baptistery was well used. We could have installed a large jacuzzi for less than the cost of a baptistery, but the PCC did not agree.

Setting up a Vision

We put together a clear vision document which was, on the whole, well received. Part of the vision was to reach out more into the community. John and Margaret Price, who had a heart for those on the edge of society set up a home for people struggling with alcohol addiction. One of the new residents, George, had a very sad story. His parents died when he was young and he was abused in the children's home he was sent to. He had ended up homeless and an alcoholic, living on the street. He started attending church with his new housemates.

One day as he was leaving the church service he told me, 'Ralph, I have given my life to the Lord.' Two weeks later he unexpectedly passed away. In my prayers I asked the Lord why and I felt Him saying, 'I wanted him to come home, for he has suffered enough.' At his funeral, the church was packed with rich people, street people and even some ambulance men, who regularly took him to hospital when he was found drunk, and once when was injured after someone had bashed him over the head with a bottle. As George's story was told by his brother there was not a dry eye in the church.

One Eleven

There were a number of young single men in the church and I felt the Lord calling me to invite some of them to meet with me on a regular basis. It came out of Romans 1:11-12:

'I long to see you so that I may impart to you some spiritual gift to make you strong that is, that you and I may be mutually encouraged by each other's faith.'

When I reflected with Fran who should be invited, we came up with eleven names. We used to meet once a month for breakfast and talked about many issues of life. I am pleased to see that all these men are going on with the Lord and most of them have gone on to be leaders in their churches.

Evangelistic Events

We had a great inter-denominational group which I led with Ken Shelley, leader of a local New Frontiers church. The demography of Harrow changed a great deal during the four years I was there. The Asian community grew from eighteen per cent to over forty per cent during that time – a large number of whom were Hindus. We wanted to run a mission to share the Gospel with them in a relevant way. We successfully ran three.

The one that stands out in my mind is when we invited an Indian evangelist called Ram Babu to come and speak. On his last night he was teaching on the parable of the rich man and Lazarus from Luke 16:19-31. He told his story of how he grew up and, having trained as a Hindu priest, went wayward. Then he met Jesus and his life changed. He told his grandmother about the importance of knowing Jesus, but she was not interested. When she died, he travailed with the Lord regarding his grandmother and had a vision of both of them on a rickety Indian bus. When he got to the station he asked his grandmother to leave the bus with him, but she was not interested.

He then saw her on the bus heading to hell and she called out to him, 'Ram Babu, save me!' He then said that when Lazarus asked for water, Abraham replied in Luke 16:26,

'And besides all this, between us and you a great chasm has been set in place, so that those who want to go from here to you cannot, nor can anyone cross over from there to us.'

He concluded by saying that was why he had become an evangelist. When prayer ministry was offered, I estimated that around half of the 400 people who came to the meeting, responded for prayer.

Challenges in Harrow

My years in Harrow had many challenges. On one occasion I had to take the funeral service of a well-loved young teacher, who passed away leaving a young daughter and son behind. But perhaps my greatest challenge was a major pastoral child protection issue that ended up with someone in leadership in the church going to prison.

As soon as I heard of the situation I contacted the Diocesan child protection team and was very grateful for their advice and support throughout the process. They wisely advised me to prepare a written report for the press, as it may be needed. Rumours started to spread in the church. To stop speculation and rumour, I invited those with concerns to meet with me in the vicarage. A dozen mothers came and I listened to their concerns: 'How can we be sure that our children are safe?' was the gist of their questions. I explained that I could not discuss the specific details of the situation, as it was going to court, but I could promise them that the person concerned was banned by the police from coming within a mile of the church.

My saddest day in church leadership was when the case came to court and I stood with the mother of the child victim and her friend to support them. Helen stood with the wife of the accused who was also a victim. In the words of the judge, the perpetrator had betrayed the trust of the church as well as the young victim. The accused received a jail sentence. We did our best to support his wife and family, as well as the victim's mother. The story hit the headlines of our local paper. The paper foolishly gave the home address of the perpetrator who was in jail, while his family were still living at that address. The issue took up a lot of time and emotional energy.

The day after the court case, both Helen and I were still feeling traumatised, but church life does not stop. Marc Dupont arrived to stay in the vicarage and lead a weekend of teaching and ministry. It turned out to be just what we needed as the Holy Spirit met powerfully with us, washing away the trauma. Shortly after I had left with Marc to take him to the airport, Helen went into the guest room to change the bed and was met with a scene of devastation! Not only was the stripped bedding all over the floor, but lots of bees had come in through the open window and were buzzing around the room. Helen sensed God saying, 'The weekend has stirred up a hornet's nest in the spiritual realm.' Tough times were ahead!

Pain of Leadership

It's difficult to describe the months that followed. Church leadership can be a lonely place and 4 years after arriving in Harrow, following a painful meeting with the Rector, I needed time out to collect my thoughts. I was under so much stress that I could not function. Fran was so worried that she ordered a trip to the doctors. The Bishop came to visit and told me to take as long as I needed before returning to work. In the event, I only needed a couple of weeks' break. Helen and I went together for a couple of counselling sessions. These were so helpful in revealing the root cause of my stress, and that helped it to be lifted straight off me.

At that time I was reading *Secrets of the Vine* by Bruce Wilkinson. This led me to ask in my prayer time, 'Is this a time of discipline or pruning?' Had I done something wrong to bring this on myself, or was the Lord refining me? I would be lying if I said it was easy to work through this time, but I believe it helped me to grow closer to God. I held His hand even more tightly and maybe it even made me a better leader. I learnt many lessons during that time.

I believe we grow spiritually when the going is tough because we learn to depend on God even more. During painful times we have three options:

To bottle it and ignore the pain;
Or, to allow the pain to move us away from God;
Or, to allow it to bring us closer to God.

A new chorus song at the time summed it up:

'In your Name there is strength to remain,
To stand in spite of pain, in your holy Name.'

Jesus never promises us that life will be easy, but He does promise that He will remain faithful to us, no matter what we go through. I chose to come closer to God and hold tightly to His hand.

Preparing for a Move

When Ram Babu came again, he prophesied over me that I would be, 'ministering in a new Christ Church.' At the time I though he meant that changes were in the air for Christ Church, Harrow. A few months later we had a visit from John Dean, a friend with an international speaking reputation. He soon sized things up: 'Either the situation has to change or you need to move.' Helen told me later about a passage of Scripture she'd read that she felt was particularly meaningful:

'The Lord your God is bringing you into a good land – a land with streams and pools of water, with springs flowing in the valleys and hills; a land with wheat and barley, vines and fig trees, pomegranates, olive oil and honey; a land where bread will not be scarce and you will lack nothing; a land where the rocks are iron and you can dig copper out of the hills.' (Deuteronomy 8:7-9)

A stirring that God may be moving us on began, but God seemed to be saying, 'Wait!'

The Team

I invited someone to review our ministry and she met up with the staff team of Christ Church. At the end of the day she said she was not surprised by how we all felt, as there had been a lot of 'loss change' over the past few years in the church. This helped me to put things in perspective again and a weight lifted off me. God was using the gentle words of others to strengthen me during this time.

Being part of this team had proven to be a very different experience to my previous teams. The structure was very complex. There were two Parish Church Councils, one at St Paul's Church and the other a combination of two District Church Councils – Christ Church and St. Peter's. Overriding the two PCC was a Team Church Council which covered all three churches. There were times when I felt we discussed some of the main issues three times over. Soon after God moved us on, the Bishop and others began to restructure this team for the better.

For us, God had another plan in mind.

Chapter 10
Christ Church, Bayston Hill

Call to Bayston Hill

Around the time I was beginning to recognise that we were being called elsewhere, my lectionary reading 'happened' to include Deuteronomy11:10-15:

'The land you are crossing the Jordan to take possession of is a land of mountains and valleys that drinks rain from heaven. It is a land the Lord your God cares for; the eyes of the Lord your God are continually on it from the beginning of the year to its end … I will provide …. and you will eat and be satisfied.'

I felt that God was promising us something good. As I meditated on it, I was given a picture of three hilly peaks which I later drew for Helen. Could these represent the Father, Son and Holy Spirit, I wondered? The overriding sense I had was that God was doing something new and somehow the hills were part of it.

A month after I had that vision I received an email from the Bishop suggesting I consider a church near Shrewsbury, which was described as a possible 'Ralph-shaped job'. Did that mean dark, cuddly and balding? As I mentioned in the previous chapter, I had spent a year preparing the church in Harrow to move towards becoming a 'cell church' and it appeared that Christ Church, Bayston Hill, had already started moving in that direction.

I asked a number of people to pray for me as I applied and the response back from all of them was very positive. One of the people I rang was my old friend John Fieldsend.

'Which church is it in Shrewsbury?' he asked.

'I don't know, some Hill!' I said as I fumbled through the paperwork. When I found it I said, 'It's Christ Church, Bayston Hill.'

It turned out that he himself had been the vicar there for over twenty years!

'I knew you should apply,' he said. 'I nearly invited you to do so, but prayed God would lead you to it. Go for it.'

I discovered later that I was in fact their third Messianic Vicar. Over the last 50 years there was a Revd Mullerman (Messianic Jew), followed by Revd Griffin, followed by my friend Revd John Fieldsend (another Messianic Jew), then Revd Griffiths and then me, Revd Goldenberg, the third Messianic Vicar. It must be the only Anglican church to have had three Messianic Vicars!

My application was last minute, but arrived just in time for the deadline. I was short listed and invited with two others to attend for interview. We had never been to Shropshire before, but as we approached Bayston Hill, on the last few miles of the journey, we were captivated by the stunning scenery.

On the second day of the 2-day interview, Helen and I were taken for a drive up to the local Bayston Hill viewpoint. There, as we turned a corner, we saw three hills spread out in front of us, exactly as I had seen in my vision. Helen and I exchanged knowing looks across the back seat of the car. All I could think was, 'Wow! Thank you, God, for showing me so clearly where my next ministry should be.' That was back in June 2001. The rest is history. I was invited to be the incumbent Vicar of the church. It is interesting that some years later we met the other two excellent candidates and they both they knew the job was for me. Both were happily settled in new posts.

Over the nine years we were in Bayston Hill, we saw some amazing things happen among a group of lovely, generous-hearted people. We were excited to be in God's will, seeing Him water those hilly peaks from heaven with His Holy Spirit. There's was a sense that God had His hand on us. After the first service, someone quickly ushered me outside to look at the sky. Just above the church was what looked like an upside down rainbow. Was God smiling over us?

TLC

Prayer and prophecy were valued gifts amongst many in the congregation. I was given a word by a number of people quoting Zechariah 8:23:

'This is what the Lord Almighty says: "In those days ten people from all languages and nations will take firm hold of one Jew by the hem of his robe and say, 'Let us go with you, because we have heard that God is with you.'"'

In fact, one person subsequently gave me a picture depicting that scripture, with the verse written in Hebrew. I knew the Lord wanted me to have a team around me who would pray with me and help me seek the Lord's will. As we were a cell church we named the team 'The Leadership Cell' which became known as TLC. Ten people, men and women, were invited to join me to form TLC.

As there was a sensitive historic pastoral issue involving safe-guarding, I felt that we should have the two elected churchwardens in TLC, which meant that whenever new churchwardens were elected they joined TLC. We also included the administrator and whoever was co-ordinating the cell groups. I tried to choose the remaining members on the basis of the 'fivefold' ministries written about in Ephesians 4:11:

'So Christ himself gave the apostles, the prophets, the evangelists, the pastors and teachers.'

I also felt that someone other than me should look after TLC, organising the meetings and leading the Bible studies. I asked Duncan Headley, in whom I recognised the fullness of the Holy Spirit. When I came for the interview I was told by the administrator Joyce Malins that Duncan was not well, so we went together, prayed and anointed him for healing. Throughout our time in Bayston Hill, despite health challenges, Duncan kept well enough to lead TLC with sensitivity and wisdom.

It became our practice as TLC for three of us to visit and pray for sick members of the congregation in response to the command in James 5:14, *'Is anyone among you sick? Let them call the elders of the church to pray over them and anoint them with oil in the name of the Lord.'*

It was also a safe place for me to share honestly and reflect where God was leading us. I was greatly blessed to have loyal and supportive churchwardens throughout my time there and I thank the Lord for each one of them.

Six years after my arrival, Bob Jackson came to review our church ministry. He first joined us for a meal at TLC. Afterwards he said that, 'One of the signs of a growing church is when the leaders can relax and have fun together and I see that in TLC.' We really did become close friends as a group.

Formulating the Vision and Mission Statement

Soon after I arrived I invited the leaders on the church council and the members of TLC to an away day to assist me in putting together our vision and mission statements. We felt that our main vision should be 'Growing the Kingdom of God in Bayston Hill and beyond'. We were given the picture of a vine with roots and 4 branches.

The roots presented 'Growing deeper in passion for Jesus'. The 4 branches presented:

- Growing closer to each other
- Growing as Jesus-Followers (disciples)
- Growing in caring for the needy (in community)
- Growing in numbers

During the away day someone asked about how prayer fitted into the picture. He wondered whether the sap of the tree could become 'Growing in Prayers'. As a biology teacher he explained that when there is sunlight, the leaves send down sap, but when it is dark they draw sap up from the roots (Jesus). That seemed right to all of us (and the Holy Spirit).

We organised a weekend away for the whole church – the first time this had happened for a long time – and I undertook to teach further on the 6 areas of our vision. It was a lot of fun for all who came and produced a great foundation for our time in Bayston Hill.

Areas We Focused on to Fulfil the Vision

1. Cells:

Part of the vision was to continue developing as a cell church. We encouraged the small groups (cells) to be more outward looking. Our model was to have clusters, each made up of six cells. It proved quite difficult persuading successful cells to multiply. We only managed to multiply one cell, but we did multiply the clusters twice. We ended up with three clusters of six cells each. Peter Stokes, who headed the cell church, arranged an evening meeting three times a year. The meeting started with an hour dedicated to the cluster leaders, then the cell leaders were invited to join us. I saw it as a time for building up the troops and sharing vision.

2. Freedom in Christ (FIC):

Another part of the vision was to encourage people in their discipleship journey and help them to walk in freedom. We had used 'Free to be' and 'Wholeness in Christ' in Harrow, but chose 'Freedom in Christ' as our main resource in Bayston Hill. We were impressed by its scriptural foundation: 'You shall know the Truth and the Truth shall set you free.' Sue Lyndsey, a member of our church and a counsellor in a GP's practice, had a real heart for FIC. She became responsible for organising intercession for the FIC UK branch of this international ministry and was later very involved in their ministry of 'Walking with the wounded'. Through her, we invited Dr Neil Anderson, who developed FIC, to speak and lead a conference in our church. Sue ran regular FIC teaching once a term. Many people went through the teaching and received much healing as they were set free by embracing truth.

3. Alpha:

We also agreed to make Alpha both an evangelistic and a foundation resource, as a means of bringing people to faith. Richard and Ann Landsdale ran our initial Alpha courses.

One of the first participants was a young mum who had come to enquire about baptism for her youngest child. We invited her to the vicarage for two sessions of preparation. The first evening her mother came with her. We explained simply what baptism meant, God's salvation plan and the promises she would be making to God on behalf of her child.

At the end of the session, Helen asked her if it had been helpful. She replied, 'I'm shocked! I had no idea what it meant to be a Christian. I need to think about it before I go further.' We suggested that the Alpha course, starting in ten days' time, might help in her deliberations. She and her mother joined the course. She became a Christian and her mother's faith was revitalised. Over the next couple of Alphas, all three of her sisters participated and came to faith.

4. Training and equipping the wider Church:

We ran a variety of training courses to equip the church in different ministries, in the church and beyond, including:

Prayer Ministry. We had a Prayer Ministry Team who met regularly to discuss our ethos, values and re-affirm our guidelines. They were available to pray with people after every service, and from the beginning there was a powerful anointing when people came forward for prayer. God was blessing His hungry people.

Worship Leaders Meetings were started by our curate, Adrian Stone, when he joined us almost two years after our arrival. Adrian was a gifted worship leader who gave much encouragement to aid the expansion and equipping of our worship teams. When Adrian left Simon Jones took over and continued the training and oversight of the worship teams.

Pastoral Ministry Meetings were organised by our licensed

LPA (Lay Pastoral Assistant) and she gathered her team together for training and encouragement three times a year. This team organised our annual service, to which we invited the bereaved relatives of those whose funerals had been conducted by the church.

Preaching. I have a heart to release others in preaching and encouraged those in whom I recognised this gift. It has been thrilling to witness young people stepping out in this gift. The most memorable was a young lady of just fifteen years old who preached with a conviction and clarity that challenged us all.

Youth Group

'So what are you going to do about it?'

Phil Extance, father of two teenagers, asked this question very soon after my arrival. He explained that there had been a steady drift of young people away from the church, as there was no group for them to belong to beyond the age of 13. Coincidentally, the first visitors to the vicarage, whilst we were still unpacking, were a young engaged couple, Matt and Cathy. They shared their heart for young people and it was clear they were already enjoying good relationships with the teens in the church. They expressed their desire to help in a more formal way with the youth and shared that they were feeling a future call to fulltime ministry.

With Helen's help, Matt and Cathy started a youth group with ten young people which we hosted. Once again our house was filled with young people on a Sunday afternoon.

We had much fun together, including sorting out the vicarage garden. In our formal meetings I often brought a 'scenario' for discussion. For example: *what should you do when your mum orders you to tidy your bedroom?* We had fun discussing how we each have a right to be free to do what we want in our bedroom space. When I posed the question of why their mums would want their bedrooms clean and tidy, the teens' imaginations went into overdrive as they thought of the worst possible scenarios. Discarded clothes and forgotten food could cause a smell and attract vermin, etc. In the ensuing weeks, parents came to us and asked, 'What have you done to our teenagers? They have been clearing and tidying their rooms!'

When Adrian arrived, he took over the responsibility of the youth group, which had grown to twenty-five, with Matt and Cathy alongside. Together they ran a youth Alpha which seventy teenagers came to. It became obvious that we needed a youth pastor. We went to the church presenting the need to finance a youth pastor and the money came in to cover at least two years. We advertised the post.

As I was leaving New Wine that summer, I got a phone call from Katie and Paul Cross, saying, 'We saw your advert on the New Wine vacancy board and want to apply for it.' I have known Katie since she was a little girl. Her parents were Clive and Sue, who were instrumental in our coming to the Lord. We also met them when they were youth pastors in a church where we took a Parish weekend. I was really pleased that they were going to apply for the job. As I already knew them, I declared an interest and stood aside from the interviewing team of five, which included a teenager. Paul and Katie were appointed on a job share basis and became youth pastors for the remainder of my time in Bayston Hill. They introduced many youth initiatives that helped grow the Kingdom of God amongst the youth in Bayston Hill.

One of these was a Youth Service at 8.00pm which was called 'L8'. 'Why L8?' I asked Paul, who informed me it meant 'late' in text language. This service allowed the evening service to continue at 6.00pm which was called 'On our knees'. It was a place where people came to be refreshed by the Lord.

L8 was entirely run and resourced by the young people and proved very effective in developing and releasing them into their spiritual gifts and ministries. It also drew in teens from smaller churches where there was no viable youth work. Young people travelled from a twenty-five mile radius, as far as Market Drayton in the north, to Ludlow in Hereford Diocese to the south.

The L8 services started with half an hour of worship, then a coffee break, followed by the preach and ministry. The lateness of the finishing time concerned parents and made us rethink. We settled for a 7.00pm service alternating between 'L8' and 'On our knees'. This had the bonus of adults and teens benefitting from each other's gifts as they joined the different services.

Some years later I met a young lady who belonged to a neighbouring church, but often worshipped and preached in our L8 service. At the time she was studying in an Elim College. She shared how those services had formed part of her spiritual journey.

Outside Ministry

I was invited to chair the Shrewsbury Night Shelter for homeless people, the Diocesan Renewal group and 'Mission Shrewsbury' – an ecumenical group of local church leaders. Each had their challenges and blessings.

The Night Shelter was the most challenging experience and included having to deal with a suicide in the building. Even so, I was greatly blessed to see how many people were grateful for the work done by the Night Shelter. In one of our AGMs, one Night Shelter user asked if he could say something. I was pleased for him to speak. He said, 'Ralph, do thank the churches who send us gifts, but can I tell you that what we really want are fingerless gloves, writing pads and envelopes.'

I was challenged that we can sometimes give people what we think they need rather than asking them what they *actually* need. So from then on, whenever a church offered to give something to the Night Shelter, we asked its users whether they needed those items.

The Diocesan Renewal Group's main annual event was an invitation to the whole diocese to a day of worship and teaching in the cathedral. I was first involved in heading up the prayer ministry and was then asked to lead it. We were really blessed by our Bishop, Jonathan Gledhill, who encouraged and attended all the events. In time, we added an evening celebration specifically for the youth, which they much appreciated. Many testimonies resulted from these events as the presence of the Holy Spirit met with God's people.

Mission Shrewsbury was an ecumenical group which I fully supported. When I was invited to take over chairing the group, I felt strongly that the leaders should meet once a month to pray for each other and be a prayer covering for Shrewsbury. It was so encouraging to see the nine busy church leaders committing to those morning meetings, to be blessed in our fellowship together and see the fruit of our prayers. We organised regular joint celebration services which moved around the different denominational churches and were eagerly anticipated as the wider family of God in Shrewsbury worshipped together.

Challenging Issues

It is easy to write about successful events, but all those in ministry know there are always challenges to be faced when leading a church. I had what I call the 'brown envelope' letters – letters, often in brown envelopes, slipped through our letter box on a Monday morning, complaining about the volume of music, or the service being too long, or some other detail that the person felt needed to be brought to my attention. There were many trivial complaints. For example, some did not like the colour of paint we chose for the walls, or the strength of the coffee that was being served.

My most challenging issue was a pastoral one involving a significant member of the congregation. I remember being approached by him one morning as I left the morning prayer meeting with Helen and my curate. He told me angrily that I should leave. He even wrote to the Bishop. I spent many hours on my knees crying out to God to show me how to handle this situation. To this day, I do not know what I could have done differently and I still carry the pain of that time and pray for that person, who I loved dearly. It subsequently turned out that he required medical treatment and care.

Ministry has a cost emotionally and spiritually, but thanks be to God who gives us the victory through our Lord Jesus Christ.

Personal Spiritual Battle

There were many situations which felt like a spiritual battle. The most challenging one was a personal one, when one of my sons wrote saying he did not want any further contact with us. We told him clearly that we loved him and always would, no matter what he did or said. We felt we had no choice but to accept his decision.

I spent many private hours praying for him and crying out to the Lord to bring our prodigal son back to us.

One Sunday, Helen had a severe cold and stayed in bed. We had a baptism in church followed by a shared meal. As I sat next to a prayerful elderly man named George, he asked me, 'How is your wayward son?' I replied 'He is still wayward, George'. He said, 'I will pray for his return soon.' As I walked into our home the phone rang and it was our prodigal son – O what joy! I passed the phone to his mum. He wanted us to have his address and to be in contact again. His subsequent marriage was the only one, out of our three sons, at which I officiated. The parable of the prodigal son has a personal meaning for me now. I now know what it means to have the prodigal son come home to his father.

Presence of God

From the beginning, God often allowed us to experience His tangible presence in many of our services. Three particular occasions stand out.

On my first Pentecost Sunday, as I woke up in the morning, I felt the Lord calling me to invite people to come forward for the laying on of hands and anointing with oil, with the words, 'Receive the gift of the Holy Spirit on this Pentecost Sunday.' At the 9.00am service half the congregation came forward. At the main 10.30am service a large number came forward and some 'rested in the Spirit'.

By the time the evening service began, it was packed with everyone in eager expectation. It was half term and parents turned up with their children, as there was no school the next day. There was a tremendous sense of the intimacy of God as we worshipped Him with great joy, and a strong anointing on the preaching about the Holy Spirit. The invitation to receive more of the Holy Spirit was given again and nearly everyone responded. The Holy Spirit was resting on everyone.

That night I saw something which I have never seen before or since. Whole families 'resting in the Spirit' in total synchronised fashion. One family, who had 4 children, all 'rested in the Spirit' in a perfect unity. I smiled as I observed the eldest son still had his hands in his pockets as he went down. As the children were filled with the Spirit they got up and spontaneously started praying and prophesying over the adults. It was beautiful to see the whole family of God ministering to each other across the generations, even though in human terms it was quite disorganised and some may even say messy. When we finally returned to the vicarage and looked at the clock, we were amazed to see how long the service had lasted – but as we later discovered, no one ever complains about the time when they are caught up in God's presence!

Over the years, we experimented with different prayer initiatives. First, we invited the church to a couple of 24-hour, non-stop days of prayer, which proved physically tiring, but spiritually uplifting.

During our first Lent, after teaching on different types of fasting, I invited the church to join me in fasting in a way that was appropriate for each person. We also set up opportunities for people to gather together in prayer.

As I recognised those who had intercessory gifts, we gathered a small group to oversee the prayer life of the church. Helen was part of this group. Out of this grew occasional half nights of prayer and then the monthly 'On our knees' evening service, mentioned earlier, focusing on worship, listening to God and intercession for the church.

Occasionally I invited the church to a week of prayer and fasting. Prayer meetings were arranged three or four times a day around a passage of Scripture, with a theme for each day, and different people were invited to lead as God guided. This led to a rich variety in style and creativity and a fresh enthusiasm for prayer. During one of these weeks, God's presence was very strong in every prayer meeting. One evening we were praying when a lady came in breathless. She said that she hadn't been intending to come, but as she sat and prayed she saw a lion cub in her hand. The cub grew bigger until it jumped over the fence, running free in Bayston Hill. She felt the Lord told that her Jesus is not a lion cub. We were making Him too small. He wanted to be all powerful in Bayston Hill!

The week ended with everyone gathering on a Saturday evening. At the end of one of those weeks Helen had a vision to set up the church in such a way that it represented Ezekiel's vision of the river of life flowing out from the temple. In the chancel area, the bishop's chair was placed in front of the communion table to represent the throne of God. From under it, flowed several metres of blue chiffon across the platform and down the steps into the worship area as the river of life. Two areas of floor in the chancel were strewn with different coloured flags – red to represent the anointing by the Holy Spirit for ministry, and green to represent leaves for healing. We invited people into 'the river' to be refreshed or to receive prayer for healing or equipping in the red or green areas.

For several weeks afterwards, we kept the chancel area set up in this way and people regularly spent time with God in the river of life.

On my last Pentecost service in Bayston Hill, we had a full immersion baptism booked for the evening service. I woke up in the morning sensing the Lord saying that we should open the pool to all those who want to be baptised. I talked it through with Helen and she replied with her favourite saying, 'Do whatever God is telling you.' As I walked into the church, Paul, our youth pastor, came up to me saying that he felt God had told him the same thing. I preached on the Ethiopian Eunuch (or was he Sudanese?) from Acts 6:36:

'As they travelled along the road, they came to ***some water*** *and the eunuch said, "Look, here is* ***water****. What can stand in the way of my being baptized?"'*

I invited anyone who wanted to be baptised to speak to me during our coffee break. I also said that if they were under 18, they must have their parents' permission. Six youngsters requested to be baptised during the break. They phoned their parents asking for a change of outfit and those under 18 handed me the phone to speak to their parents. I also heard the youngsters phoning their friends saying, 'God is here, come quickly!' Suddenly the church was packed. I made sure they knew what they were doing and they all agreed to be followed up by our youth ministers.

During the coffee break, parents and friends arrived. One mother, a midwife, was about to go to work, and requested that we baptise her daughter first.

Following the baptisms, we had our time of worship with people receiving the gifts of tongues and others experiencing a fresh touch of the Holy Spirit. The service which started at 7.00pm finished after 11.00pm. As I walked home around 11.20 pm, I was wondering why the Lord was calling me to retire? I felt Him say that this was His parting gift to me for my time in Bayston Hill.

Goodbye

I retired in June 2010. How sad it is to say goodbye to much loved people whose lives you have been intimately involved with, through both times of joy and sorrow. The church gave Helen and I a wonderful send-off. On the Saturday we had a great family party with a BBQ and many expressions of love. Then on the Sunday, as I led the 9.00am and 10.30am services and gave out the communion bread I was feeling very tearful. Helen held it together at the first service until they all laid hands on us at the end. Then during the coffee break there were tearful hugs as older members of the first service said their goodbyes.

She composed herself for the next service and all was well until she was helping serve the wine. She came to one man who had tears streaming down his face and this set her off again. Paul and Katie's son, Zac, immediately sized up the situation and followed Helen around with a box of tissues!

I looked into people's eyes and just wanted to hug each one and thank them for all that they had given me and Helen. I pray that I was able to contribute in a little way to their journey with the Lord.

Chapter 11
A New Chapter in the Adventure With Jesus

Start of a New Chapter

I recently heard that someone who was approaching retirement was thinking of what should be put on his tombstone. For me it was different, I was excited to know what the Lord had planned for us next.

When I was a young Christian we used to sing, 'It's an adventure following Jesus.' It certainly has been an adventure so far, with Jesus holding our hands. As I retired and moved south, back to Ferndown, I was thinking, 'What next Lord?' I felt the Lord saying that for 6 months I was to make no decisions. It was not simply that I was tired and needed a rest, although I was grateful for that, but more the sense that God had a plan for us. It was hard, however, waking up each morning with nothing in my diary! We vicars feel an empty diary could mean God is not using us. I am learning an empty diary means He can feed me with His presence. What more could one ask for?

As I prepared to retire, many requests came flying in from different places. One of them was the request to apply to a church in St. Raphael, who had a vacancy for a Chaplain. In fact, someone from the church phoned while we were in the midst of packing. When he heard what we were doing, he suggested I should address the boxes to St. Raphael in France! But I didn't apply as they were interviewing in December 2010, only 5 months after I retired, and God had spoken so clearly about not making any decisions for 6 months. This turned out to be right and in the end they chose a Chaplain who committed himself to lead the church for the next 5 years. However, when he retired and the chaplaincy was vacant once more, I stood in the gap for part of the interregnum.

During those first 6 months of retirement, we visited a number of churches in the area, including St Mary's Church, Ferndown, where I was a churchwarden, and St Andrew's, Kinson, where I did my first curacy. Both Helen and I felt that God didn't want us to return to where we had worshipped before.

One Sunday we went to the Lantern Church in Merley, about fifteen minutes' drive from home. Wow! We knew immediately it was where God wanted us to be. It felt like home. We were welcomed by the vicar's daughter and met two members of our former church in Harrow who had retired to Merley. The worship style was just like we enjoyed in Bayston Hill. We hit it off with Andy Rimmer, the vicar, and his wife, Mary. In fact, when Andy went on Sabbatical two years later, I covered the Sunday services and supported the staff team in any way I could. Helen and I were asked to head the Prayer Ministry team, which we did for three years. I still enjoy ministering to, and sharing with, the lovely people in the Lantern. I occasionally preach and lead in their midweek and Sunday services.

To My Jewish Friends

All through my time serving Jesus as my Messiah, I have met many Jews who have been searching for truth. Recently, an Orthodox Jew came to me. He had come to realise that Jesus had actually walked on the earth and had a real connection with God. He knew that Jesus was a Jew who kept the whole law of God and all the feasts. Now he had a burning desire to know whether Jesus was not just a godly man, but a divine being, YHWH Himself, and if Jesus really is the long-awaited Messiah. He needed to know how much of his Orthodox Jewish rituals were still relevant to serving God.

As I have grown to know the Lord and been on my own journey, I have found my Jewish roots to be foundational in my relationship with God. I looked at this man, at the start of his journey of discovering that God does not want to be distant and hidden in a list of rules, but longs for us to have a living relationship with Him, like Adam in the Garden of Eden. In this man, I could see myself. Living by the grace of God, I no longer have to follow the rabbinic laws to be accepted by God, but I have never stopped being Jewish.

My final prayer for all who read this book is from Ephesians 3:14-21:

'For this reason I kneel before the Father, from whom every family in heaven and on earth derives its name. I pray that out of his glorious riches he may strengthen you with power through His Spirit in your inner being, so that Christ may dwell in your hearts through faith. And I pray that you, being rooted and established in love, may have power, together with all the Lord's holy people, to grasp how wide and long and high and deep is the love of Christ, and to know this love that surpasses knowledge – that you may be filled to the measure of all the fullness of God. Now to him who is able to do immeasurably more than all we ask or imagine, according to his power that is at work within us, to him be glory in the church and in Christ Jesus throughout all generations, for ever and ever! Amen.'

The only advice I could give him is the same advice that had rung in my ears; the same advice that I encourage all who read this book to take:

Seek the truth and when you find it, lock it in your heart.

CMJ

I was invited to re-join the Council of CMJ (Church's Ministry Among Jewish People) UK four years ago. As I prayed about it, I felt it was right to be part of this wonderful ministry. CMJ's values – the three E's – represent where my heart is:

Evangelism: The Great Commandment of Jesus for all believers is to make disciples:

'Therefore go and make disciples of all nations, baptizing them in the name of the Father and of the Son and of the Holy Spirit.' (Matthew 28:19)

Paul affirms the Great Commandment and makes clear the order to whom we are to share the Gospel in Romans 1:16:

'For I am not ashamed of the gospel, because it is the power of God that brings salvation to everyone who believes: first to the Jew, then the gentile.'

It is important to note that the Great Commandment is not only to the Jews, but to all people on earth.

Education: Whenever and wherever I share the Gospel and its Jewish roots, people get excited. Part of our teaching is not only to reaffirm our Jewish roots, but to say that God has not finished with the Jews. He still has a plan for them.

Encouragement: We all need encouragement and much more so when we are going through difficult times. CMJ is able to encourage many people on their spiritual journey, especially those who have Jewish roots. My prayer is that this book will be of help to those searching for truth, and that through Jesus the

Messiah, Yeshua Meshach, they will come into a relationship with God the Father, Son and Holy Spirit.

In retirement I am enjoying the varied experience of preaching in many churches, both Anglican and Baptist. It is such fun seeing the Lord using me and Helen in our retirement. I used to say to the Lord, 'Here I am, Lord, send him or her.' Now I say, 'Send *me* wherever you want me to go!'

Now is not the end. It is really an adventure following Jesus.

Addendum 1
Saying Goodbyes

Final Thoughts

The sad part of retirement years is saying goodbye to dear friends, especially those who have been significant on our life's journey.

Over the years, following my time in Kinson, Vic suffered several serious, life-threatening illnesses. On the evening of 18th December 2015, I knew I had to visit Vic in Poole Hospital. It wasn't an ideal evening. Helen's brother had undergone major heart surgery earlier that day in Southampton Hospital and his wife was staying with us, so we could care for her and take her to visit during his stay in hospital. However, I *knew* I had to visit Vic that night. I put on my vicar's collar so that I could visit out of hours. Vic was seriously ill. We had a special time praying together which I will never forget. His son Mark was present.

I was prompted by God to read a psalm. Vic said it meant a lot to him. I then anointed him with oil and left late at night. Later that night he passed away and went to be in glory with His Lord. Once again, I learnt the importance of responding to the prompting of the Holy Spirit and the blessing of being where God wants me to be.

It was a real privilege to be invited by Jill to preach at his funeral service in St Mary's Church, Ferndown. I preached from the Psalm I'd shared with Vic:

'You have searched me, Lord, and you know me. You know when I sit and when I rise; you perceive my thoughts from afar You discern my going out and my lying down; you are familiar with all my ways. Before a word is on my tongue you, Lord, know it completely. You hem me in behind and before, and you lay your hand upon me. Such knowledge is too wonderful for me, too lofty for me to attain.' (Psalm 139:1-6)

'Who is Vic?' I asked his family, friends and former colleagues who had gathered to pay their final respects. Then I shared what Vic meant to me: the perfect role model of a godly man, a caring pastor, a wonderful teacher and expositor of God's Word, and a great church leader. I learnt so much from him when I was his curate in Kinson and have tried to emulate him in my years in church leadership. He was truly the perfect training incumbent.

Vic's friendship, together with Jill's, has meant a lot to Helen and me. I loved his humour, his smile, his wisdom and his encouragement. I loved being with him and enjoying his fellowship.

I drew out 3 points which described Vic:

1. An evangelist who preached the Word (2 Timothy 4:2,5)
2. Vic loved Jesus and knew nothing would separate him from His Love (Romans 8:37-39)
3. Vic's certain hope in the resurrection of Jesus as His Lord (John 11:25) was a challenge to all of us.

Goodbye, my friend Vic. I still miss you.

Colin Bedford also passed away to be with his Lord some years ago, soon after he retired. Sadly, I was unable to attend his funeral in December 2014, but I wrote the following tribute to him to be read at his funeral:

'I first met Colin when I was interviewed for the position of curate in charge of St Andrew's and was subsequently accepted to be part of the Edgware staff team. Colin was larger than life in may ways – joyful, full of energy (in spite of the fact that he had diabetes) – and blessed Helen and I greatly during our time in Edgware.

His zeal for the Lord and God's Word always shone through and he touched many lives around him. This is not only because he set up and ran 'Bedford Bookshop', but he loved to read God's Word, expound it and share it. He had an incredible gift of soaking up information and was able to read at a fast rate. I remember one Alpha evening when he sat at the back with a book in his hand, saying he had read 60 pages during the evening. I commented that was a page a minute. His reply, with a twinkle in his eye, was, 'That was a bit slow, wasn't it.' In all our staff meetings we reflected on God's Word and learned much from Colin.'

Our staff meetings were full of fun and laughter and I wondered whether June ever thought we did any work, besides laughing as a team. Colin also had a lovely sense of humour and he didn't mind us teasing him. He often told stories of how he knew different people who, by some coincidence, always seemed to be staying in the room next to him when he went away to one place or another. So we invented this joke about him.

'Colin seemed to know everybody. One day he said to his staff that he would be meeting Tony Blair, who had the room next door to him. To prove it, the staff could stand outside Number 10 and watch him go in and out. It happened just as Colin said it would. He said the same thing about the Queen, which also came true. When he said he knew the Pope, the staff went to Rome and stood in the Vatican Square as instructed by Colin, to see him coming out on the balcony next to the Pope. The staff didn't know the Pope and they wanted to make sure it really was him, so they asked the Roman Catholic Priest standing next to them whether that really was the Pope standing on the balcony. The Priest answered, 'I'm not sure if that is the Pope, but I can tell you that's Colin Bedford standing next to him – I'm staying in the room next door to him.'

Colin fell about laughing when he heard this and enjoyed the joke immensely. Funnier still was when we heard that he had met someone on holiday in France whose brother had the desk next to Colin's brother at school!

Colin was also a great encourager. I greatly miss his fellowship, his depth of understanding of the Word of God and his love of Jesus. But I know he now has a mansion in heaven and I hope that one day I'll have the room next door to him!

Then there is Fran. A loyal friend, a wise confidante, and always ready and able to manage any crisis. She was fun to be with and full of the Holy Spirit. Her last few years were lived in the knowledge that her life may be cut short, but she never stopped serving the Lord, right up to the end. The overflowing church at her funeral was a tribute to all the lives she influenced by the way she lived her life. Well done, good and faithful servant. I still miss you.

Addendum 2
Celebrating the Jewish Feasts

The rhythm of the Jewish feasts was an important part of my upbringing and is still a key part of who I am. My memories of them help to define where I have come from. My understanding of them helps to bring alive my faith in *Yeshua*, Jesus. I am so thankful for the added richness I gain from the Gospels as I read how Jesus celebrated them with His disciples and I think about my own personal experience of celebrating the feasts. As I share my insights with others, often people's eyes light up as they say, 'I never saw that before!'

As I think of the memories I have from each of the feasts, I realise how important they are to me in my faith journey.

Shabbat Leviticus 23:3

Looking back, I find myself reflecting on the richness of the Jewish home liturgy and rhythm of life, especially on the Shabbat (Sabbath). The Shabbat day starts at sunset every Friday. What a wonderful thought for a healthy rhythm of life to start the day at sunset (*'There was evening and there was morning'* Genesis 1:5) with rest and then sleep halfway through the day and, in the morning, go out to work! So different from being exhausted after work. Our work should be out of a place of rest.

The Shabbat liturgy includes the *Berakha* – the blessing of the family – and the *Kiddush* –sanctifying the wine and bread that is shared with the whole family, including the children who are part of the covenant. How many Christians have family prayers at Sunday lunch after church? There is so much we can learn from our Jewish roots that can strengthen and bless family life.

Purim: Book of Esther

Purim is a typical example of how Jewish festivals become party-time! It is celebrated around February. The Jews were commanded to relive the Old Testament story of Esther with a day of joy (*simkha*), feasting and giving presents (Esther 9:19). I loved the wonderful sweet foods offered in the feast, including the traditional 'Haman's ears' which were made from triangles of pastry, sweetened with dates and honey, to represent the ears of Haman, the villain of the story.

We celebrated together the landmark edict from King Xerxes to allow the Jewish people to defend themselves from attack by enemies and to take the spoils of war. The present giving included giving to charity. The story is still told and retold in homes every year. So what did we do in our family?

Our extended family would all gather together for a big party to hear the story retold. The children all wore fancy dress. I can remember being a cowboy, chasing after my brother who was dressed as an Indian, while my sister dressed up as an eastern princess, looking on at us all.

We would clap and cheer whenever Esther or Mordecai were mentioned, then boo loudly for Haman. I was confused whenever King Xerexes was mentioned – to start with he was booed when he killed Queen Vashti and then cheered when he supported Esther. This feast involved so much joy and laughter as we shared together as a family.

Three Harvests!

The rhythm of the religious year for Jews is heavily dependent on the agricultural calendar, in much the same way as the Christian tradition celebrates harvest. The Jews celebrate three harvests, one for each different batch of crops!

- Passover/*pesach*: around Easter, April/May – the first harvest
- Pentecost/*shavuot*: May/June – the mid harvest
- Tabernacles/*sukot*: September/October – the final harvest, celebrated by the 7-day Feast of Tabernacles

Pessach: Leviticus 23:4-14

Why celebrate Pessach?

The name *Pessach* comes from the 10th plague, when the Lord passed over Egypt and the native firstborn children and animals died, but the Jewish homes were protected by the blood of the sacrificial lamb, daubed on their doorposts, as the angel of death passed over them. It was only then that Pharaoh was miraculously convinced that he should give the Jews their freedom to leave Egypt. So the whole of the Passover is an exuberant celebration of God's protection, in saving and liberating His chosen people. The story is recorded in Exodus 12:11-20:

'This is how you are to eat it: with your cloak tucked into your belt, your sandals on your feet and your staff in your hand. Eat it in haste; it is the Lord*'s Passover. "On that same night I will pass through Egypt and strike down every firstborn – both men*

and animals – and I will bring judgment on all the gods of Egypt. I am the Lord. *The blood will be a sign for you on the houses where you are; and when I see the blood, I will pass over you. No destructive plague will touch you when I strike Egypt. This is a day you are to commemorate; for the generations to come you shall celebrate it as a festival to the* Lord *– a lasting ordinance. For seven days you are to eat bread made without yeast. On the first day remove the yeast from your houses, for whoever eats anything with yeast in it from the first day through the seventh must be cut off from Israel. On the first day hold a sacred assembly, and another one on the seventh day. Do no work at all on these days, except to prepare food for everyone to eat – that is all you may do. Celebrate the Feast of Unleavened Bread, because it was on this very day that I brought your divisions out of Egypt. Celebrate this day as a lasting ordinance for the generations to come. In the first month you are to eat bread made without yeast, from the evening of the fourteenth day until the evening of the twenty-first day. For seven days no yeast is to be found in your houses. And whoever eats anything with yeast in it must be cut off from the community of Israel, whether he is an alien or native-born. Eat nothing made with yeast. Wherever you live, you must eat unleavened bread.'"*

Even as a child I always had a sense of incredulity at Passover. Of all the feasts, this one was the best, surrounded with a special awe. There was something very special, too, about the way that the children were encouraged to ask questions: 'Why… why… why?" I remember asking my Rabbi Jewish teacher, 'Why did God need the Jews to paint blood on their doorposts? Surely He knew that their names were written in the Book of Life?' Now I understand that we need to play our part too: God chose to use the Jews, even though He could have carried out His purposes without them. Obviously the questioning habit stuck, because I found myself still doing it in my head years later!

Pessach requires the consumption of bread which is unleavened only as a reminder of the hurried way that the Israelites had to prepare to leave Egypt once the word was given. So the night before, mother disposed of all the leavened bread in the house, except for one piece, which she hid. Then it was the job of Dad and me (as the youngest child) to hunt it down and burn it. Whoever found the *Affikomen* or *Tzafun* (the hidden one) was given a prize.

The first night of Passover meal was celebrated at home. The meal traditionally consisted of egg mayonnaise followed by roasted chicken stuffed with rice and dried fruits. During the meal the story of the salvation of the Jews is told. The first night ritual is called *Haggada Seder* or the 'Order of Narration' for Haggadah is 'telling the story' and Seder is 'order of service'. It is generally accepted that the Last Supper was a *Haggada Seder* celebrated by Jesus, the Jewish Rabbi, with His *Talmidiem* (disciples).

The *Haggadah* (telling the story) *Seder* (order of service) is a lot more than a harvest supper. The whole meal is crammed full of visual aids – most of them the edible kind! So there are eggs to represent new birth; bitter herbs as a reminder of suffering and salt-water representing tears; a shank-bone symbolises the sacrificial lamb. There's even a special brown paste made from dates, apple, red wine and almonds to represent the bricks made without straw. Four cups of wine accompany the storytelling, with drops of wine spilled to represent each plague.

At the start of the service Mum had to light the candles. There's something really beautiful about the prayer that a woman says:

'The people who walked in darkness have seen a great light. On those who lived in the land of the shadow of death, the light has shone down.' (Isaiah 9:2)

It is said a woman, Eve, first brought the darkness into the world by eating forbidden fruit, and so has to light the candles to usher light into the darkness. Isn't it incredible that it was also a woman, Mary, who gave birth to the Light of the World on the first Christmas day!

As I was the youngest child in our family, I read the *Ha Mishtana* (4 questions) and listened carefully to the answers. The story of how God delivered my ancestors from the oppression and slave labour of Egypt was very special to me. The 10 plagues and the miracle of dividing the sea were marvellous to me as a child and I was spellbound every year as I heard about them. This took us neatly to one of the other aspects of *Pessach*. It's a festival of redemption that looks both backwards and forwards. *Pessach* celebrates God's final deliverance of Israel from Egypt, and especially the protection of their firstborn on the night of Passover.

It is also a reminder of the future coming of the Messiah. The Jews firmly believe that this 'Messianic Age' will be heralded by the return of Elijah, so an empty place is laid at the table for Elijah to come. I remember a real sense of awe on that first night of *Pessach* when we opened the door to await the coming of Elijah. Would tonight be the start of the Messianic Age? It is in this context that Jesus said,

'"But I tell you, Elijah has already come, and they did not recognise him, but have done to him everything they wished. In the same way, the Son of Man is going to suffer at their hands." Then the disciples understood that he was talking to them about John the Baptist.' (Matthew 17:12,13).

There are certainly indications that John the Baptist was indeed born at or around the time of Passover in March. We read in Luke 1:5 that Zechariah was in the temple performing his priestly duty as he was in the line of Abijah. In 1 Chronicles 24:10 we see that the line of Abijah was on the rota for the 8th week after 1st Nissan (April) i.e. June. If Elizabeth got pregnant in June, then John would have arrived around Passover time (March/April). It is also interesting that when Mary was visited by the Holy Spirit and went to visit Elizabeth, we are told that Elizabeth was 6-months pregnant (December), so the most likely date for the arrival of Jesus would be September or Sukot Tabernacles – the very time of the year that Jews expect the Messiah to come. This led to another of my questions: *Why do we celebrate the birth of Jesus in December?*

Celebrating Pessach in the 70s in the UK With Family

In the late 70s Dad and Irma, my stepmother, invited Helen, our 3 boys and me to a Passover meal. Irma had a tradition of having a hard-boiled egg in salt water for starters. My 3 boys could not eat them and I found myself having to eat 4 boiled eggs, secretly taking one of each of the children's eggs whenever Irma left the room and Dad was not looking. It put me off boiled eggs for a long time!

There's something very special for me about the Passover. After I met with Jesus, we celebrated Passover with my brother, Sol, in London in 1982. I will never forget that day. When the door was opened to allow Elijah to come in and join the feast, the cat walked in. This made us all smile. When the cat walked straight to Elijah's seat round the table and sat down we all burst into laughter.

It was also during this celebration, as a fairly new Christian, that my passion was awakened to plug the Christian faith back into its Jewish roots. It's a connection that can give Christians a better understanding of Jesus, His life, His times and His teaching. After all, it was Jesus Himself who said in Matthew 5:17, *'Do not think I have come to abolish the Law or the Prophets; I have not come to abolish but to fulfil them.'* If I had to choose only one feast to demonstrate the transition of the Old to the New Covenant, it would be the feast of Passover.

As the ceremony unfolded I began seeing it in a new light. There was a real continuity between my Jewish roots and my newly discovered relationship with Yeshua, Jesus, my Messiah. It all came alive that evening in a new way as I began to grasp the big picture of God's story – His-story. Following that evening I felt the Lord guiding me to put together a Jewish Passover which included the New Testament teaching. I called it 'Haggadah of the True Lamb'.

As I put the booklet together, I felt the Spirit of God showing me something about the three *matzos* and the symbolic way they are used in the Passover meal: piled one on top of the other in 3 pockets. There are various different Jewish traditions to explain what the 3 *matzos* stand for. For example, some Jews claim that they represent Abraham, Isaac and Jacob. Others say they represent God, the priestly tribes and the Jewish people. But as I was taken in the Spirit I felt the Lord showing me the 3 *matzos* as God the Trinity, with Father at the top, Son in the middle and Holy Spirit at the bottom. Many other Messianic Jews have also been given this insight.

As I looked at the Passover liturgy I came to believe that Jesus was breaking the middle matzah (representing Himself) as He said, *'Take and eat, this is my body.'*

In today's liturgy one half is replaced in the middle pouch.

This half is taken jointly with the top half (Son and Father coming together) before the third *matzah* (the Holy Spirit) is eaten as a sandwich to be shared by everyone. The other half (the *affikomen* or *tzafun*) is hidden during the meal to be searched for at the end of the meal by the children. Whoever finds it is given a gift. How appropriate! If we come to Jesus as a little child, we are given the gift of the Holy Spirit.

There are other striking parallels too. It is interesting that the first cup of wine after the supper is known as 'the cup of salvation'. *'After supper He took the cup...'*, we read in the story of the last supper. *'This cup,'* Jesus goes on to say, *'is the new covenant in my blood.'* Jesus gives a new meaning to the cup of salvation: our salvation comes through His shed blood. For Christians, Easter is a time when we can focus on the cross and grasp the New Covenant of God's powerful act of salvation, just as a Jew would focus and remember God's powerful act of salvation through the Exodus from Egypt.

Jews celebrating the Passover meal lean to the left when eating and drinking. This symbolises being free people who can lean to the left, with the right hand unencumbered to eat in freedom. How much more should we who are free in Jesus joyfully demonstrate our freedom!

It's sad that the Christian Synod of Laodicea in the 4th Century separated the two festivals of Passover and Easter, with the result that the Jewish Passover, as observed by the Jews in the last supper, is no longer followed in most Christian homes.

Shavuot – Weeks – Pentecost: Leviticus 23:15-22

The Hebrew word *Shavuot* is plural meaning 'weeks'. It is celebrated by Jews as a commemoration of the Ten Commandments being given to Moses on Mount Sinai, as well as being the second harvest festival. It is to take place 7 weeks after *Pessach* on the 50th day, from which it gets its Greek name, Pentecost.

It's a popular time for weddings, too. At my nephew's wedding the Rabbi reminded the bride and groom of their responsibility as 'People of the Book', to place God's Word in the centre of their lives. I think it's no coincidence that it was Pentecost when the Holy Spirit came in power on the first Christians (Acts 2).

I've heard it said that as Christians if we depend only on the Word without the Spirit we *dry up*; on the Spirit but not the Word and we *blow up*; but if we have the Word and the Spirit in balance we *grow up*. That is exactly the message of *Shavuot*. God's timing in giving His Word to Moses and after Jesus' ascension coming as the Holy Spirit!

Rosh Hashanah: Leviticus 23:23-25

The Jewish month of *Tisheri* begins with the ritual sounding of rams' horns (*shofars*) as a herald of God's message. When I was a child the haunting sound of the *shofar* being blown seemed to go beyond hearing it in my ears or even my head. It felt as if it reached deep into my soul. I could visualise myself in the Rabbi's shoes calling the people into battle.

There are ten days of ritual cleansing and repentance ('days of penitence'). This period is symbolised in different ways by different groups of Jews. In Edgware you could always tell when it was Rosh Hashanah by the scraps of paper fastened to lamp-posts round the town. The Jews had written their sins down and posted them there. Elsewhere Jews might screw up the pieces of paper and throw them into a river or the sea. The important thing is to use the time to purify oneself from sin. In

Israel, the bits of paper are placed in the cracks of the Wailing Wall in Jerusalem.

Yom Kippur: Leviticus 23:26-32

Just nine days after Rosh Hashanah the 24-hour fast of *Yom Kippur*, the Day of Atonement, is celebrated. In the heat of the Sudan, that meant we would have a dry mouth and extreme thirst, especially by the afternoon. When I was thirteen, I used to debate with my peers around this time. If we clean our teeth are we having a small drink and so breaking the fast? Are we allowed to clean our teeth? What about washing our face? If that not only cleans our face but also eases our suffering, are we allowed to do this during the fast?

Yom Kippur was one of the last ritual Jewish observances I held on to, even after Helen and I were married. It was a way in which I felt I could earn forgiveness for my sins. By this suffering I was somehow nearer to God. Yet it never truly satisfied me. Now I believe I am forgiven through Jesus. I no longer fast for my sins to be forgiven so that God will forgive me. Instead, I fast when the Holy Spirit guides me to, especially when there's a need for a spiritual battle. It's a way of showing God that I'm serious that supercharges my prayers and sharpens my spiritual antennae!

Sukkot – Tabernacles: Leviticus 33-44

Tabernacles falls on the 15th day of the Jewish month of *Tisheri* around September or October. It is preceded by the 2 other major feasts, *Rosh Hashanah* and *Yom Kippur*. *Tisheri* is the holiest and busiest month in a Jewish household. I remember my mother being busy with many preparations, especially food. Whilst she was busy I would skulk around in the backyard behind the garage to keep well out of the way. I didn't want to be under my mother's feet as she rushed around preparing everything.

Just three days after the Day of Atonement, *Sukkot* begins and lasts for seven days. Our Christian Harvest happens around the same time. It celebrates the final harvest of the agricultural year. Tradition has it that each day the High Priest drew water from the healing Pool of Siloam to pour on the altar, to invoke a blessing over the following year's crop. But it's also a reminder of the provision by *YHWH* of shelter and food for the children of Israel during their 40 years in the wilderness.

In Jesus' day, on all the major festivals, Jews would have travelled to Jerusalem. Now each household shares together in the building of a *Sukah* shelter. We did this when I was a child. It was great fun – a bit like a family decorating the Christmas tree. Palm branches were collected to build the *sukkah* and as much fruit as we could get hold of to hang from the top. As we ate our meals, listening to the story of how God provided for Israel always sent a thrill down my spine and still does. The shelter felt like a very special privilege. In fact, the *Sukkah* is the only *Mitzvah* blessing in which we are completely surrounded, from head to toe, by the *Mitzvah* itself – enveloped, as it were, in the Divine presence. So now when I read in John1:14 that, '*The Word became flesh and made his dwelling* (Greek: *Eskunessen Sukkah*) *among us,*' I can picture Jesus enveloping me!

Choel Ha'Moed

The half way point of the week of Sukkot is called Chol Ha'Moed. Some believe it is the most likely day when the Messiah is to come. As I reasoned earlier, Sukkot is the most likely time when Jesus was born. I read in John 7:14, '*Not until halfway through the festival did Jesus go up to the temple courts and begin to teach.'* Was that on *Chol Ha'Moed?*

Simchat Torah

The 7th day of *Sukkot* is called *Hoshana Rabba* when the final portions of the Torah are read. This is followed by *Simchat Torah*, a day of rejoicing filled with *Rouach Hakodesh* (Holy Spirit). This gives insight into Jesus teaching in John 3:37-39:

'On the last and greatest day of the festival, Jesus stood and said in a loud voice, "Let anyone who is thirsty come to me and drink. Whoever believes in me, as Scripture has said, rivers of living water will flow from within them." By this he meant the Spirit, whom those who believed in him were later to receive. Up to that time the Spirit had not been given, since Jesus had not yet been glorified.'

Hanukah: John10:22

Hanukah is the Festival of light or Dedication which is celebrated in December. It commemorates the miraculous success of the Macabean revolt which liberated the enemy-occupied temple. The story goes on to say that as the temple was cleansed, ready to be used again for worship, there was only enough of the sacred oil to keep the Menorah candelabra in the temple burning for one day, Miraculously, the Menorah remained alight for eight days giving time for a fresh batch of sacred oil to be prepared.

To commemorate this festival a special *Hanukah* candelabra is used. It bears eight candles and a removable *Shemesh* (servant) candle. On the first evening one candle is lit using the servant candle. Then each day one more candle is lit, until all eight candles are alight on the eighth day.

For children, this is a very exciting festival as they take turns to use the servant light to light the candles, with the added bonus of a present each day for eight consecutive days! The servant light reminds me of Jesus coming as the Light of the World and the presents, the gifts of the Holy Spirit available for us daily when we submit our lives to the Servant King, Jesus.